Pakistan in the Eye of a Thunderstorm

Military, Secret Agencies and Politics of Alliance Making

Pakistan in the Eye of a Thunderstorm

Military, Secret Agencies and Politics of Alliance Making

Musa Khan Jalalzai

Vij Books India Pvt Ltd

New Delhi (India)

Published by

Vij Books India Pvt Ltd
(Publishers, Distributors & Importers)
2/19, Ansari Road
Delhi – 110 002
Phone: 91-11-43596460
Mobile: 98110 94883
e-mail: contact@vijpublishing.com
www.vijbooks.in

ISBN: 978-93-93499-91-2 (Hardback)
ISBN: 978-93-93499-96-7 (Paperback)

Contents

Introduction

In 2003, an Assistant Director of Inter-Services Intelligence (ISI) Lahore office once told me: "Regretfully, we were secretly spying (watching) on you for more than six months, in order to discover your possible links to foreign intelligence agencies, but luckily, our intelligence report authenticated your sacrosanctity and blessedness ". By calling on the carpet, I regretted and suspired that their intentions were inhospitable. I was in full consternation that they might harm me abruptly. By and by, I arrived at a conclusion to leave Pakistan for my homeland-Afghanistan. But regrettably and sad to say, managements of the Inter-Services Intelligence (ISI), Intelligence Bureau (IB), Naval Intelligence and offices of Inspectors Generals in four provinces never recognized and acknowledged hundreds of my theses for the promotion and advancement of Brigadiers, Major Generals, the ISI high-ranking officers, Naval Intelligence commanders, SSP rank officers, DIGs, and Inspector Generals of Police. Worse luck, I received no payment and remittance of my writings, because I was living in Pakistan as a refugee and a homeless person. (This Author).

In July 2022, a military commando critically and dangerously tortured political analyst, columnist and TV commentator, Ayaz Amir in front of Dunya Television headquarter in Pakistan, to teach him a lesson for criticizing political interference of military establishment and intelligence agencies in government. Editor of Friday Times, Najam Sethi, in his editorial page (15 July 2022) noted: "The bad news is that, despite such condemnation, this despicable practice continues with impunity because no civilian government has the courage or wherewithal to put an end to it. The good news is that, despite the overhanging threats, more and more people are being so bold as to speak their mind on the subject. The elephant in the room decidedly looms ever so darkly but is no longer sacred or invisible. This is unprecedented. Under the developing circumstances, we should not be surprised to see the developing nexus between the Judiciary and Miltablishment forcefully extended into the future. This will be a true measure of the hybrid nature of future civilian regimes rather than just the relationship between the civilian rulers and the Miltablishment".[1] Mr. Ayaz told a local journalist (The Nation, 02 July 2022) that his vehicle was blocked and nearly six people tortured him and his driver. The attackers reportedly were wearing face masks. Social media also shared pictures of journalist Ayaz Amir, who suffered injuries. Former Prime Minister Imran Khan condemned the incident along with several journalists and TV pundits.[2]

Journalist Ayaz Amir (Hindustan Times, 02 July 2022) was returning home after recording his television show for Dunya News TV channel, where he worked as a senior analyst when unknown persons stopped his car. The attackers manhandled him and tortured his driver before fleeing the scene. With bruises on his face, Amir said that the masked men not only "hit him and tore his clothes, they also took away his cell phone and wallet". They left when people started gathering on the busy road". Pictures circulating on Twitter showed the journalist sitting in a car with his shirt torn. In a tweet later, Ayaz Amir said those who attacked him did not care about his age. "I have no personal enmity with anyone and I had no quarrel with anyone. Whoever attacked me didn't even care about my age," he said. "The only fault was that I speak the truth and I will continue to speak, God willing," he said in another tweet. Hindustan Times reported.[3] Former Prime Minister in his tweet condemned humiliation and torture of Ayaz Amir. "I condemn in strongest terms the violence against senior journalist Ayaz Amir today in Lahore. Pak descends into the worst kind of fascism with violence and fake FIRs against journalists, opposition politicians, and citizens. When the State loses all moral authority, it resorts to violence". Pakistan National Commission for Human Rights (NCHR) said in a statement that the attack showed that journalists in Pakistan were losing ground and that this was against the constitutional right to freedom of expression.[4]

The Inspector General of Punjab (IGP) also took notice of the incident and directed CCPO Bilal Siddique Kamyana and DIG Operations Sohail Chaudhry to take immediate action. SP Civil Lines Safdar Kazmi visited the crime scene and met the victim at the TV office. The CCPO said the police would ensure the arrest of the accused as soon as possible with the help of CCTV cameras. Prime Minister Shehbaz Sharif also condemned the incident and ordered Punjab Chief Minister Hamza Shehbaz to hold a high-level investigation. "Suspects should be brought before the law as soon as possible. Journalism and protection of journalists should be ensured," said PM Shehbaz. The Association of Electronic Media Editors and News Directors (AEMEND) also denounced the attack. "The attack on respected journalist Ayaz Amir speaks of grave conditions journalists face in Pakistan".[5] On 21 April 2022, the Committee to Protect Journalists noted a group of around 20 PTI workers assaulted Khawar Mughal, a reporter for the privately-owned broadcaster 92 News, at a party at the Minar-i-Pakistan monument in Lahore, the capital of the northeast Punjab province. Attacks on journalists began in July 2022 when gunmen in Khairpur district Sindh fatally shot local reporter Ishtiaq Sodharo. The slain man was associated with a local Sindhi-language weekly. His wife accused an area police officer of ordering the deadly attack against her husband. The motive for the killing was not known.[6]

A day later, Iftikhar Ahmed, a reporter for the Urdu-language national Daily Express, was ambushed and killed by unknown gunmen in north western Khyber Pakhtunkhwa. The International Federation of Journalists condemned the killings. "Pakistan's government must take appropriate measures to ensure journalists' safety and security, as required by law and act to reduce assaults on journalists so that they may carry out their work without fear". International Federation of Journalists warned.[7] Moreover, police also arrested journalist Imran Riaz Khan in Islamabad in connection with a treason case registered against him. He was detained for criticizing and highlighting the military's alleged role in Pakistani politics. Tracking Civic Space (Monitor-16, 08 2022) reported the Federal Investigation Agency (FIA) initiation of a criminal inquiry against journalist Sami Ibrahim for allegedly transmitting "anti-state" videos and statements on various social media platforms. The inquiry was initiated under the controversial Section 20 of the Prevention of Electronic Crimes Act (PECA) 2016, part of which was struck down by the Islamabad High Court (IHC). The FIA, in a press release, accused Ibrahim of being "involved in spreading fake news regarding state institutions".[8] The office of the Director-General of the Ministry of Information and Broadcasting's External Publicity Wing told CPJ that Abraham appeared to violate Article 19 of the Pakistani constitution, which restricts freedom of speech on the basis of the "integrity, security or defence of Pakistan", which relates to a video published on 2nd May 2022. In that video, Abraham discussed an alleged foreign conspiracy to oust former Prime Minister Imran Khan, who was removed from power in a no-confidence vote on 10th April. Monitor noted.[9]

Journalist and expert Sanskriti Bhatnagar, in his commentary (Press freedom in Pakistan has the latest casualty the arrest of ARY News journalist: Pakistan ranks 157 on the Reporters Without Border's Press Freedom Index of 2022, below war-torn Afghanistan and Russia, the Print, 10 August, 2022) has noted torture and killing of journalists and media workers in Pakistan: "Journalists in Pakistan are regularly subjected to trolling online and violence offline. In February 2022, Mohsin Baig, editor for the news outlet Online and a vocal critic of the government, was arrested for making "obscene" remarks about Imran Khan. In May 2022, Pakistani police launched criminal proceedings against at least six journalists and talk show hosts for "spreading hate against the army and state institutions in their reporting."[10] In July 2022, two journalists were killed, a columnist was tortured, and the police arrested an anchor of a political show on YouTube - all in the span of one week. Pakistan has also ranked ninth for two consecutive years (2020, 2021) on the Global Impunity Index, which assesses countries where journalists are regularly murdered and their assailants go free. According to reports, 138 Pakistani media professionals lost their lives in the line of duty between 1990 and 2020".[12]

Torture and sexual abuse by Pakistani intelligence agencies, military establishment and police in prisons and secret cells has become an unwritten law in Pakistan, where thousands innocent and powerless citizens have lost their lives. Military establishment recently kidnapped Professor Shahbaz Gill and crippled him by using unlawful methods of torture. He was first raped and then physically abused. Former Prime Minister claimed that Professor Gill was subjected to sexual abuse. On 19 August 2022, journalist Rizwan Shahzad reported former Prime Minister Imran Khan's statement, in which he claimed that his chief of staff, Dr. Shahbaz Gill was sexually abused, vowing that he would leave no stone unturned to bring to justice those who were responsible for mentally and physically torturing his aide. Announcing taking out a rally against the alleged torture on his aide facing charges of inciting mutiny in the army, the PTI chairman said that he had obtained detailed information about the "inhuman treatment" meted out to Gill and questioned "who tortured Gill", especially, when the capital's police said it did not inflict any torture. Rizwan reported.[13]

After seeing photos and videos showing Gill gasping for air while being taken to the court and hospital, the PTI chairman went to meet Gill at the Pakistan Institute of Medical Sciences (PIMS) but was denied permission. Talking to the media at PIMS, the former PM said that if a political worker can be tortured, one could imagine what an ordinary citizen goes through; adding that such "inhuman treatment" and "torture of a political worker" was unacceptable. "All the pictures & videos show clearly [Shahbaz] Gill was tortured both mentally & physically incl[uding] sexual abuse-most too gruesome to relate. He was humiliated to break him down," Imran tweeted while sharing a video of Gill wherein he pleaded for an oxygen mask. While questioning who tortured Gill, Imran, without specifically naming anyone, stated that "there is a general perception in public at large and in our minds too as to who could have carried out the gruesome torture", warning "remember the public will react". Subsequently, Imran vowed to leave "no stone unturned to find out those [who are] responsible and bring them to justice." Express Tribune (18 August 2022) reported.[14] Moreover, on 19 August 2022, Imran Khan was denied permission to meet Shahbaz Gill at the hospital. "We will conduct rallies across all divisional headquarters," Khan said, inviting PTI supporters to join him in raising his voice against the torture and ill-treatment meted out to his chief of staff. "They don't care about court orders," he said, criticising the government's treatment of Gill and their disregard in relation to his health. Journalist, editor and analyst, Najam Sethi in his editorial comment (15 August 2022) noted TV statement of Shahbaz Gill:

"Imran Khan's Chief of Staff, Shahbaz Gill, recently went on ARY TV to provoke, knowingly and wilfully (as he has admitted), officers of the armed forces not to obey "illegal" orders of the high command in support of "evil". Why did he do so, knowing well that the Miltablishment would consider it tantamount to provoking mutiny and rebellion in the armed forces, whose consequences could potentially lead to a court martial and severe punishment? Why did the Miltablishment opt to arrest him instead of rapping him on the knuckles through a strong warning statement from ISPR. But then how come there was no strong objection from the same quarters when a lower court judge quickly remanded him to judicial custody after only two days in police custody for investigation and interrogation? The questions keep coming. Why did Imran Khan shift the venue of his August 13th Jalsa from Islamabad to Lahore? Why didn't he blast the "neutrals" or target the Americans for "changing his regime" as he has done so thunderously in the recent past? Indeed, why didn't he back up Shahbaz Gill's statement, confining himself only to the "unfair" arrest and "brutal" treatment meted out to him? Instead, considering how popular he thinks he is, why is he so worried about what lies in store for him? Why has he come to terms with the fact that a quick election is not in the cards? Why is he so worried that he may be disqualified from contesting elections for not being "Sadiq and Ameen" in consequence of the screaming revelations in the Prohibited Funding Report released by the Election Commission of Pakistan? The answers are blowing in the wind. The Miltablishment has sent Imran Khan its assessment and advice going forward."[15]

MM News (15 August 2022) reported humiliation and torture of Shahbaz Gill in captivity. Gill was arrested at Banigala Chowk in the capital after a video clip of his controversial remarks went viral on social media. In an interview with journalist Fereeha M Idrees on GNN News, Imran Khan said that he was "extremely upset" with the treatment meted out at Gill in prison. "It is extremely painful. I didn't even know this [...] our lawyers told us that his clothes were stripped off and he was beaten up. "They are torturing and trying to mentally break him. And they are forcing him to give statements against Imran Khan," the ex-premier alleged, adding that if "Imran has to say something, he will say it himself [...] he doesn't need Shahbaz Gill for that". He further revealed that Gill was asked about "Imran and Lieutenant General Faiz Hameed's meetings".[16] The Punjab government removed DIG Prison Rawalpindi Region and Adiala Jail superintendent from their positions after the PTI alleged that Dr Shahbaz Gill was being tortured at the jail. WION TV channel in its report (18 August 2022) noted Imran Khan's argument that Pakistan was 'descending into a banana republic'. "The civilised world will be shocked at our levels of barbarism," tweeted Imran Khan, along with a video of Gill being transported to the hospital. "The worst part is an easy target has been chosen to make an example of through torture and without a fair trial." WION Channel reported.[17] Voicing concern about Shahbaz Gill being detained again, the PTI chief alleged that Gill's arrest was a conspiracy to target him and his party. "He is in a fragile state of mental and physical health because of the torture inflicted on him when he was abducted and taken to an undisclosed location and then again at the police station. This is part of a conspiracy to target me and PTI by forcibly getting false statements against us similar to what they have been doing against social media activists," he said.1 Wion TV Channel reported.[18]

Tehrik Insaf filed petition in Islamabad High court against the Gill's torture. The petitioner pleaded for the formation of a medical board to conduct the medical examination of the PTI leader Gill by unbiased doctors. While talking to media, Asad Umar said that due to the breathing issue, Shahbaz Gill was admitted to Pakistan Institute of Medical Sciences (PIMS) Islamabad. He said that as per the law, no one can be tortured like this. On 18 August 2022, Doctors said that Imran Khan's aide needed assessment by specialists following torture accusations. Journalist Aamir Saeed reported recommendation of the medical board at the Pakistan Institute of Medical Sciences (PIMS) in Islamabad that Dr Shahbaz Gill, the chief of staff of ex-premier Imran Khan needed to be examined by a cardiologist and a pulmonologist, following accusations by the Pakistan Tehreek-e-Insaf

(PTI) that he had been tortured in police custody while under arrest on sedition and incitement to mutiny charges. Gill was brought to PIMS from Adiala Jail in Rawalpindi for a check-up after Islamabad police took over his custody following a court ordering a two-day physical remand. However, Dawn (18 August 2022) reported Imran Khan's statement that warned military establishment to "review their policies" while there was still time. "I want to ask the neutrals today [...] do you know where the country is heading?" he said during his address at a seminar in Islamabad. "How can the country and economy progress when you don't even know what will happen in the next 2-3 months," Imran asked, adding that political stability was the prerequisite for economic development and neither could be had without free and fair elections.[19]

Human Rights Watch (HRW) called on Pakistani lawmakers to speed up the adoption of a bill that criminalizes the use of torture; a practice that the rights group said was widespread in Pakistan. "Justice and accountability in cases of torture will only be possible if parliament passes the torture bill and the government enforces the law by carrying out transparent and impartial investigations into torture allegations." "Tightening government restrictions on freedom of expression and association in Pakistan has gone hand-in-hand with increased violence against journalists, activists, and religious minorities," said Patricia Gossman, associate Asia director at Human Rights Watch. "The government needs to reverse course in 2022 or the human rights situation will continue to plummet." HRW said. In February 2022, five officials of Pakistan's Intelligence Bureau (IB) were suspended after a popular television presenter and journalist Syed Iqrarul Hassan accused them of torturing him.

Pakistan's Inter-Services Intelligence (ISI) and civilian intelligence agencies in mollycoddling and wrecking the image of Pakistan in the international community raised several questions including political involvement of the country's army in politics and alliance making. Army Chief General Qamar Bajwa has been involved in a massive corruption cases including the purchase of land and a big house in Belgium, where he has intended to shift along with his family after retirement. By reading his corruption saga and violation of human rights in Baluchistan and Waziristan, the Canadian Parliamentarian, Tom Kmiec accused him for supporting terrorist groups. Visiting Canada, General Qamar Javed Bajwa came under heated criticism in the Canadian Parliament. Mr. Tom Kmiec who slammed his government for approving the amount of $50,000 for COAS Bajwa's reception from the taxpayer money of Canada. Mr. Kmiec said Bajwa was accused of toppling two civilian governments. Adding that military under his command was accused of human rights abuses, and extrajudicial killings, and has deep links to terrorist groups.[20] Tom Kmiec, a member of Canada's Conservative Party, made those remarks against Bajwa in the House of Commons, the lower house of the Canadian parliament.

General Bajwa exhibits special interest in the incarceration of Ali Wazir. Ali Wazir, a member of the National Assembly, was incarcerated in December 31, 2020, in several cases that accused him of hate speech, sedition and inciting the public against the state. In November 2021, Pakistan's Supreme Court granted Wazir post-arrest bail in one of these cases, but in view of the other cases against him, he remained incarcerated. Wazir's latest application for bail was dismissed on February 15, 2022, by an anti-terrorism court in Karachi due to the Bajwa involvement in his case. On 12 May, 2022, Muslim League leader, Maryam Nawaz warned that the army chief must have a flawless image. She criticised former Chief of ISI, Faiz Hameed for his political role in orchestrating her conviction in a corruption case. Maryam Nawaz also hammered the Pakistan army for war crimes in Balochistan. Baloch's are suppressed, killed and subjected to enforced disappearance by the ISI and the army by the day. That being the case, ISI and the Army lost public confidence due to their political role, and their involvement in massive corruption cases. Their loyalty to the state is in question, they dismembered Pakistan. People, an important constituent of the elements that define a State, are fast losing faith in their military and intelligence institutions that kill their own people, loot their houses, and destroy their properties. The point is that the Inter-Service Intelligence (ISI) lacks adequate intelligence information collection experience from remote areas of Balochistan, Sindh and Waziristan. The agency lacks trained manpower, fails to understand modern technology, it lacks proper intelligence-sharing approach with policymakers, and lacks a technique of actionable intelligence.

Newspaper Dawn reported agreement of PTI and PMLN (Rare consensus among rivals on ISI's role in civilian setup-June 4, 2022) that the country's premier spy agency, the Inter-Services Intelligence (ISI), should be under civilian control and answerable to the parliament after the PML-N-led coalition government gave the agency legal cover to screen civilian officials. PML-N leader and former information Minister Pervaiz Rasheed said on Twitter that if the ISI was being tasked with vetting civilian officials, then the spy agency should be placed under civilian control and be answerable to parliament. Former information minister and PTI leader Fawad Chaudhry agreed with Rasheed and said that if "institutions wanted to increase their role in civilian affairs, then they would have to pay for it in the form of public accountability". "The institution (ISI) has to think about what role it wants to play in Pakistan's politics. A discussion is needed on the new roles of civil institutions and institutions after the media revolution," he tweeted. Meanwhile, former Senate chairman, PPP's Raza Rabbani termed the decision to task ISI with screening civil servants "surprising", saying it amounted to "ceding civilian space". Dawn reported.[21] Moreover, Outlook Magazine of India in its report (Pakistan Government Formally Assigns Govt Officials' Screening to Spy Agency ISI-07 August 2022), noted clearance of Bureaucrats' promotion by the ISI agency:

"Pakistan's premier spy agency ISI had always informally screened and verified the country's civil servants, but Prime Minister Shehbaz Sharif has now officially tasked the Inter-Services Intelligence (ISI) with the job, providing a legal cover and formalising a job that the agency had been doing for a long time, as per a media report. The Dawn newspaper reported that Sharif had notified the DG ISI as the Special Vetting Agency (SVA) for verification and screening of all Public Office Holders (Officers Category), according to the Establishment Division notification in exercise of powers conferred on the Prime Minister. The quoted laws empower the prime minister to amend or make rules for the civil bureaucracy. The direction was issued from the office of the Prime Minister on May 6. By doing so, Sharif has given legal cover to a practice that had already been in place but had not been formalised as part of the protocol, as per the Dawn report. A senior official from the Establishment Division told Dawn on the condition of anonymity that the ISI and the Intelligence Bureau (IB) both send their reports about civil servants before they are posted on important assignments. Reports are especially sent to the Central Selection Board (CSB) at the time of promotion of bureaucrats. According to the official, notwithstanding the notification, the IB will continue to send its reports as per routine. The official said that since the government has now given legal effect to reports issued by the ISI, these could henceforth be used in courts as valid legal documents, the newspaper said. However, a former Establishment Division secretary disagreed. He noted that though the prime minister has the power to amend or make rules for the bureaucracy, it would have been better if the Establishment Division had issued a Statutory Regulatory Order (SRO) to amend the Appointments, Promotions and Transfer (APT) Rules governing the civil bureaucracy if it wanted to give the ISI formal charge of the vetting process"[22]

In the past 72 years, the Pakistan army came on the scene for the first time at a crossroad and failed to go back or take another road. Its consecutive martial law regimes mentally, physically and officially promoted a militarised culture of intelligence and easily murdered civilian culture of intelligence in the country. The army and ISI role against the government of Imran Khan has been contradictory and underwhelming. The IB (Pakistan) and ISI suffered from a lack of checks and balances, and the influence of government and private stakeholders. Shortfall of Scientific collaboration and interoperability between the ISI and civilian agencies, and intelligence agencies of neighbouring states prompted misunderstanding. The ISI and civilian agencies have been accused of shameless inability and inefficiency in handling the tottering state, particularly over the past four decades. Pakistan is, moreover, at war with itself. This partial civil war has been caused by the misadventures of many state agencies, as well as of many internal and external forces. 30% of the ISI and civilian agencies are collecting low quality intelligence information and misleading policy makers. All these forces are working on divergent agendas, with little care about the future of Pakistan's citizens and the implications of these deadly agendas for South Asia and the rest of the world. The war in neighbouring Afghanistan is weakening Pakistan as a modern state. The longer the war in Afghanistan continues, the more it will complicate the situation in Pakistan.

In view of this illegal business, the ISI lost its professional capabilities and hung in the air as a militant agency. The agency has lost public confidence and its roots emaciated in civil society. The rivalry between the IB and ISI became tense when a Joint Investigation Team (JIT) probing alleged money laundering by the Sharif family made a written complaint to the Supreme Court that the IB was wiretapping JIT members, including ISI and military intelligence personnel. The crucial question that still needs to be addressed is whether these agencies function under the watchful eyes of an elected government or are they still so sturdy that they are themselves instrumental in installing or toppling such governments. All civilian and military agencies have a specific mind set, their sectarian affiliation and dearth of electronically trained manpower, lack of professional surveillance approach, and the absence of a proper intelligence-sharing culture raised serious questions about their credibility. Pakistan's military establishment and its secret agencies have been using jihadists in Afghanistan to achieve their strategic goal. Pakistan's backed Taliban are fighting to control natural resources and sites in different provinces of Afghanistan. It was reported in May 2019 that illegal mining of gold and other precious minerals dramatically increased in Taliban controlled regions close to the border with Pakistan.

There are numerous stories of the IB and ISI successes and failures as agencies faced condemnation from politicians and civil society due to their sarcastic behaviour, enforced disappearances and political involvement. The intelligence cycle is a structured process, to gather information, converting it into relevant intelligence, and pass it to those who require it–the decision-makers, but the ISI and civilian intelligence agencies of Pakistan have painted a new picture of intelligence cycle by sharing state secrets with political, sectarian and religious stakeholders in order to justify their loyalties. There is an impression in Pakistani media that the ISI has become a state within a state, where no real check and balance existed to oversee its enforced disappearance and business of illegal harassment. The failure of Inter-Services Intelligence to intercept consecutive terror attacks on Pakistan, and its intransigence to maintain professional intelligence cooperation with civilian intelligence agencies raised many questions. The list of problems faced by the Pakistani intelligence machine is long. This unreformed and unchecked secret machine has suffered numerous diseases and forced it to demonstrate like a schizophrenic and a batty man.

The Inter-Services Intelligence and Military Intelligence lack of trust has been a long-standing concern in civilian circles. Writers and intellectuals in their forums have also raised the question of public confidence. Majority of the members of intelligence agencies of the country belong to different sectarian, ethnic, political and jihadist groups. They leak important security and intelligence information to these entities and sects. This illegal affiliation also directed intelligence operations on sectarian and ethnic bases. Poor data collection with regard to the activities of militant sectarian organizations and their networks across the country is a challenging problem. Many criminals who joined terrorist groups were not tracked and profiled effectively. Intelligence agencies of the country protect professional criminals and sectarian elements in safe houses and use them against politicians and those who criticize corruption and war crimes of the Armed Forces in Waziristan and Baluchistan. The ISI provided intelligence to Pakistani policymakers and performed several operations but extremely failed to achieve a single objective. The shrewdness and perception that ISI is the number one intelligence agency in South Asia is not accurate; the agency is weak, corrupt, politicized, and militarized, and its national security approach is controversial. It collects intelligence in an uncustomary manner, which leads policymakers in the wrong direction.

Its intelligence officers are not so greatly educated and unable to use modern intelligence technology properly. There are thousands of volunteer informers who work for the agency in different environments, but don't even know the basic knowledge of intelligence information techniques while settling political vendettas through illegal means. Their purveyed low-quality intelligence information led policymakers in the wrong direction. Well-known British Journalist, Declan Walsh in his book (The Nine Lives of Pakistan) noted some controversial aspects of the ISI demonstrations and manifestations: "While it is effective on street level. The ISI is not a professional service in the mold of the CIA or Britain's MI6. The organization is afflicted by the same bungling and corruption as the rest of the Pakistani state. It has frequently lost control of its most dangerous assets-Puppet masters who can't control their puppets," as Robert Grenier, a former CIA station chief in Islamabad, put it. "And when it comes to analysis, the ISI has a poor record. 'They saw everything through pre-determined ideological prisms, rather like the KGB during the Cold War, a senior British official who worked with the ISI for decades told me; 'Frankly,' he added. 'None of their analysis was worth the paper it was written on'. Journalist Declan Walsh noted.[23] The tug of war between ISI and the IB and their operational interests in Afghanistan is being discussed in intellectual circles in Pakistan and Europe. Their so-called sympathy with Afghans fully exposed when they started investigating Afghan men and women in their secret investigation and torture cells in all provinces of Afghanistan in 2022.

War of strength between the ISI and Intelligence Bureau (IB) has been reported time and again by Pakistani newspapers to manifest that a decade long fight of state intelligence agencies might jeopardize national security of the state that hitherto affianced with neighbours in geographical altercations. The IB headquarters in Punjab has customarily been looted and plundered by the ISI commando groups in 1980s, 1990s and 2000s, and all secret records of domestic and international intelligence information was despoiled. The rough and tumble of intelligence information technology between the two secret agencies brought shame to the country when ISI refused to share that technology with the IB management. Once, a former DG of Intelligence Bureau chronicled the real story of controversial intelligence technology in an hour-long meeting with this author in Lahore. However, my closest friend Khawar Zaman, a former Joint Director, evinced a critical document about the ISI's political demonstrations and its illegal interference in state institutions. He told this author that the ISI and military establishment bribe judges and media owners in cases of their interests. However, one of my friends, a former DG ISI, told this author that IB spied on ISI and GHQ in 1997 and 2013.

General Faiz Hameed, former DG of ISI visited Kabul in 2021 to finalize the Taliban cabinet. Inter-Services Intelligence (ISI) forced the Taliban to announce an interim government that was guaranteed to preserve ISI's control over the crankshaft of power in Kabul. The ISI also secretly announced a coalition of small jihadist groups (The Islamic Invitation Alliance) in Afghanistan, which was separated from the Taliban and the ISKP. The purpose of the formation of this alliance was to crush Taliban leadership if they refused to follow the ISI's instructions. Foreign Policy Magazine reported the Islamic Invitation Alliance (IIA) was founded in 2020 with funding from the ISI and had been on the radar of US intelligence for more than a year. General Faiz Hameed's interference in Afghanistan and the constitution of a controversial cabinet there caused his removal by Army Chief General Bajwa.

The way military intelligence operated over the past decades was not a traditional or cultural pattern. Instead of tackling national security challenges, the ISI, along with Military Intelligence (MI) and the IB unnecessarily concentrated on making political alliances and countering democratic forces within the country. When the intelligence war among military and civilian agencies intensified, the blame-game became the main focus of literary debates in newspapers and electronic media. Democratic forces stood behind civilian intelligence agencies, while pro-establishment forces supported the ISI and its undemocratic business. In 2014, officials from the ISI had their phone calls eavesdropped at the height of civil-military tension. On 13 September 2013, Dawn newspaper reported allegations of the Directorate General of Inter-Services Intelligence (ISI) against the 34 civilian inspectors who filed petitions with the Islamabad High Court (IHC) that they were compromising national security and hampered the smooth functioning of the organization as well.

War of words between the Baloch Regiment Group with the unwanted groups of sarcastic generals and formation commanders intensified. General Faiz was replaced by Lt Gen Nadeem Ahmed Anjum as the Director-General of the ISI. Faiz Hamid was deeply criticized by the leadership of Pakistan Muslim League-N in its meetings and protests for his controversial role in politics. These appointments come at a crucial time for the country's politics. Expert and journalist, Mr. Abbas Nasir has documented (14 September 2017) Pakistan's intelligence infrastructure weaknesses, lack of confidence and its growth in the size and scope of intelligence activities that might be linked to their role, but some analysts understand that Pakistan never changed the old British culture of intelligence and never tried to adopt modern intelligence and technological culture to make intelligence fit to the fight against radicalization and terrorism. Pakistan's own experience in intelligence failure is not confined to Inter-Services Intelligence (ISI), failure of civilian intelligence agencies to counter-terrorism, radicalization and political turmoil are prime examples.[24]

The number of reports and recommendations to improve the performance and operational mechanism of intelligence agencies has remained only on papers, while agencies didn't allow changing their manner of operation. On matters of foreign affairs and intelligence, the ISI and civilian intelligence failed to create a friendly environment with neighbouring states while intelligence related to national security is marked more by failures than successes is a sad reality. Intelligence war and short-term remedies all combine to lead up to flawed outcomes. Centre-provincial relationships have never been improved due to strained civil-military relations. Since the fight against insurgency in Waziristan and Baluchistan started, civilians have been wrongfully harmed in both crossfire and air force bombardments. Many of these mistakes are said to result from conflicting commands due to rivalries among security agencies. Since the rise in violent attacks perpetrated by Taliban across the country, the army failed to differentiate between terrorists and insurgents. Countless security lapses, including incidents such as attacks on the army amplified the importance of resolving intelligence failures.

Musa Khan Jalalzai,

Expert of Telepathic-Mind Control Intelligence

Geospatial Intelligence Analyst-2022

Chapter 1

Pakistan in the Eye of a Thunderstorm

Islam has often been used by Pakistani Mullahs, military establishment and political parties for their own ambitions and motivations. Every so often, Hadeiths of Prophet Muhammad (PBUH) were misquoted and misused by declaring unlawful jihad against neighbouring states. The Mullahs role in Pakistan's domestic and foreign policy has been regulated and calibrated by miltablishment and mosques have been sponsored to prepare young students for jihad. Mullahs have been interpreting and elucidating Holy Quran in accordance to their sectarian motives, justify their controversial jihad by misconstruing and misreading the words of Allah Almighty (J). In the 1990s, Mullah-military alliances defeated democratic forces and expanded the role of military establishment and intelligence infrastructure in state institutions by a besmirch campaign against democratic forces. Barelvi Mullah, Dr. Thahirul Qadri in his own rustled-up Hadeith, declared jihad (Ghazawa-e-Hind) against India in 1990s. Later on, the military establishment constituted a holy war between Sunni and Shia sects and between Barelvi and Ahl Hadieth sects to emancipate their rising military power, and then they were armed against Christian communities. The army established a pure Barelvi Tehreek-e-Labbaik to defeat democratic forces in the election. This sectarian organization is known for its protests in opposition to any change to Pakistan's blasphemy law. The late Khadim Hussain Rizvi was the leader of TLP. Tehreek-e-Labbaik was founded on 01 August 2015 by Khadim Hussain Rizvi, in Nishtar Park in Karachi.

Collaboration of Pakistan army, Inter-Services Intelligence (ISI) and civilian intelligence agencies in mollycoddling and wrecking the image of Pakistan in the international community raised several questions including political involvement of the country's army in politics and alliances making. Army Chief General Qamar Bajwa has been involved in massive corruption cases including purchase of land and a big house in Belgium, where he has intended to shift along with his family after retirement. By reading his corruption saga and violation of human rights in Baluchistan and Waziristan, Canadian Parliamentarian Tom Kmiec accused him for supporting terrorist groups. Visiting Canada, General Qamar Javed Bajwa came under heated criticism in the Canadian Parliament. Mr. Tom Kmiec slammed his government for approving the amount of $50,000 for COAS Bajwa's reception from the taxpayer money of Canada. Mr. Kmiec said Bajwa was accused of toppling two civilian governments. Adding that military under his command was accused of human rights abuses, and extrajudicial killings, and had deep links to terrorist groups. Tom Kmiec, a member of Canada's Conservative Party, made those remarks against Bajwa in the House of Commons, the lower house of the Canadian parliament. Expert and analyst, retired Indian Army Officer who has served in terrorism-infested areas of Jammu & Kashmir, Assam, Nagaland and Manipur, Nilesh Kunwar (June 26, 2022) has noted General Bajwa's corruption and his links to terrorist groups:

"While questioning the appropriateness of the Canadian Defence Ministry's decision of releasing $ 50,000 for the visit of Gen Bajwa to Canada in 2020 [which was subsequently cancelled due to COVID pandemic], Canadian Member of Parliament Tom Kmiec exposed the host of illegal activities committed under his watch by the Pakistan army. Speaking in the House of Commons, he mentioned that Gen Bajwa stands "accused of two toppling two governments of Pakistan, [and] the military under his command has been involved in human rights abuses, extrajudicial killings and has links to terror groups." By remaining in a state of perpetual denial on human right violations, extrajudicial killings by Pakistan army as well as its links to terror groups, Islamabad has abdicated its constitutional responsibility of protecting its minority communities. So, just like Rawalpindi in Mazari-Hazir case, while Islamabad too must be complimenting itself for having 'killed' the serious charges of human rights Canadian lawmaker with a démarche, such puerile attitude is only damaging Pakistan's international image and the fact that it has been languishing in the FATF grey list since June 2018, is proof of this".[1]

All generals and their cronies have been deeply involved in corruption and extrajudicial killing of Afghans and Pakistani citizens since 2001. General Bajwa's precursor, war criminal General Raheel Sharif also looted and ransacked his country. He committed war crimes in Waziristan and Yemen by killing children and kidnapped hundreds of women. General Pervez Kiyani and General Musharraf chewed their country with pointy and incisors teeth. Some generals and officers were found spying for foreign agencies and some were found involved in billions of corruption cases. Plundering a poor country and its starved population is a misdemeanour and crime. They trained suicide bombers across Asia and the Middle East, and managed the smuggling of narcotics and business of fear in Waziristan, Kashmir, Kabul and Quetta to make money and buy houses in Europe and the United States. Pakistan is in the eye of a rainstorm and all dangerous handbooks ahead are clearly marked. Civil-military relationship has deteriorated, and turmoil within the army quarters has been boiling dangerously for years. In the past 73 years, the Pakistan army and its intelligence agencies came on the scene for the first time at the crossroad and failed to go back or take another road. Its consecutive martial law regimes mentally, physically and officially promoted a militarized culture of intelligence and shamelessly murdered civilian culture of intelligence in the country. The army and ISI role against the government of Imran Khan has been contradictory and underwhelming. Global Village Space in its news analysis (29 November 2017), noted the emergence of different sectarian organizations in Pakistan, and argued that after the execution of Mumtaz Qadri, the TLYR emerged as a powerful Barelvi group. The Global Village Space analysts also noted demonstrations of TLYR its alliance with the army:

"The TLYR and its political wing, the Tehreek Labbaik Pakistan Party arose out of a popular protest movement that glorified the murder committed by Mumtaz Qadri, a bodyguard of the governor of Punjab province. The governor, Salman Taseer was gunned down by Qadri in 2011 over his attempt to interfere in a blasphemy case. As the movement progressed, it has only become more explosive. Heralding itself as a guardian of the Khatam-e-Nubuwat (Finality of Prophethood), the movement seems to have galvanized the political Barelvi element in Pakistan. After the formation of Pakistan, Maulana Abdulsattar Niazi and Maulana Shah Ahmed Noorani from the Barelvies remained in Pakistan politics but were largely restricted to only one national and two provincial constituencies. The dominance on Islamist politics and key national issues has always been the scholars of the Deoband school of thought and the semi Salafist Jamaat-e-Islami. In the past 70 years, religious pressure groups in national politics came out of the strain of Islamist ideology derogatorily called 'Wahhabis' by the Barelvis. In the recent two decades, their archrivals the Deobandis became a major factor due to the Tehreek-e-Taliban Pakistan. In order for dialogue with the TTP, the Government and the army had to reach out to the Deobandi Ulema, which led to the balance of religious political force completely shifting in favour of the Deobandis. The constant presence of the JUI-F in the last 6 Governments is a clear proof of Deobandi religio-political power."[2]

MEMRI-TV in its report (Tehreek Labbaik Ya Rasool Allah-TLY: The Islamist Movement At The Center Of Anti-Government Protests In Pakistan-November 27, 2017) has noted that the proposed amendment to Pakistan's election law that sought to dilute an oath requiring candidates to declare that Muhammad was the last prophet generated controversies: "The amendment was scrubbed due to protests by Islamic clerics. While protests by Islamic clerics are not new, what is new this time was the emergence of a new group of Islamic clerics united under Tehreek Labbaik Ya Rasool Allah (TLY), which were both a religious movement and a political party. It was led by wheelchair-bound Islamic cleric Maulvi Khadim Hussain Rizvi, who belongs to the Barelvi school of Sunni Islam, a so-called pro-Sufism peaceful school of Islam".[3]

The emergence of religious groups suchlike TLP and Lashkar-e-Toiba was a good opportunity for military establishment and intelligence infrastructure to challenge political leadership in Pakistan. Pakistan army protected its alliance with sectarian mafia groups to challenge domestic governance of India and Afghanistan. We have seen in the past Mullahs fight against the military establishment on several fronts, but after violent crackdown by the army, several groups joined religious parties. In Red Mosque-Islamabad, the army killed 2500 innocent madrassa students and a brother of Mullah Abdul Aziz. In 2017 and 2018, the Faizabad dharna of the TLP leadership sponsored by the army raised many questions including the army involvement in anti-state business. The TLP leadership figured out how to decapitate the faux authority of the Pakistani state so that they could announce that there was a new Capo in town. Expert and analyst, Mosharraf Zaidi in his column (How TLP won 2017, 2018, 2020 and 2021: Since the Faizabad dharna, the TLP leadership has figured out a formula that makes their speeches, their Facebook posts and their WhatsApp messages more powerful-The News, 02 November, 2021) noted some aspects of TLP and the killing of Punjab Governor Salman Taseer by his own bodyguard and issue of FATF's grey list:

"The Tehreek-e-Labbaik Pakistan (TLP) is the most Pakistani of all Pakistani political parties. It has lived the lives and archetypes of all that have come before it, and any that may come after. Sparked by a compelling and unassailable top-line narrative, supported by powerful stakeholders within the state as an implement to weaken an already entrenched political group, and now a fully grown, vastly uncontrollable 'adult' Frankenstein's monster that inhales the ecosystem that bred it in the first place. Growing like cancer, organically, as it consumes all the unwitting molecules of normalcy that bend their knee before it, in supple prostration. Relishing the most recent capitulation of the Pakistani state to the TLP is a strange but understandable instinct for the pro-democracy types whose stomachs churned at the sight of the manner in which the Faizabad dharna of 2017 was used to settle scores with the PML-N government of the day. The Imran Khan fan club in the most elite of spaces and among powerful stakeholders has shrunk since back in 2017–but lessons are never learnt if a price is never paid"......Salmaan Taseer didn't know it then, but standing up for Aasia Bibi's legal right to defend herself against blasphemy allegations was the unwitting spark that lit the fuse in a society that, back in 2011, was still racking up jet black terrorism body count, and preparing for a generation of PTSD public policy in which all that decision-makers can see is red (that is the red of Pakistan's balance sheet, and the grey of the FATF's grey list).[4]

The Dawn Newspaper (06 February 2019) reported threats, abuse, provoking and promoting hatred of the leaders of Faizabad dharna: "The media provided unabated coverage to TLP. Anyone having a grouse against the government joined in. The report submitted by Inter-Services Intelligence (ISI) under the title 'Public Support' and subtitle 'Political Parties/Personalities' listed the following: Sheikh Rasheed Ahmed, Chairman AML, Ejaz-ul-Haq, PML-Z, PTI Ulema Wing Islamabad released audio message, Sheikh Hameed (PPP). The free publicity made TLP, a little-known political party, into a phenomenon. Basking in the limelight, TLP's leadership became ever more intransigent, abusive and aggressive". Dawn reported.[5] Political analyst and expert, Imaan Zainab Mazari in her commentary (TLP Saga: How Govt Nurtured Those It Is Terming 'Militants' Today: If the government is sincere in cleaning up the mess it gladly participated in creating when it suited its political objectives, it must now start from the implementation of the Faizabad dharna judgment in letter and spirit-30 October 30, 2021, The Friday Times) highlighted the TLP saga and government support to the militant groups:

"Director General of the ISPR, Major General Asif Ghafoor, gave media briefings accusing the Pashtun Tahafuz Movement (PTM) of receiving foreign funding. Let us not forget that all this has taken place in the aftermath of the Faizabad dharna judgment (Suo Moto Case No. 7/2017). All those shots were fired by those who have always been above regulation but as usual, in the wrong direction. In paragraph 32 of the judgment, the Supreme Court observed: "The Election Commission's report states that

TLP did not provide information about its funding despite repeatedly directing it to do so." At paragraph 42 of the judgment, it is clearly stated that when the Inter-Services Intelligence (ISI) was asked by the court whether the TLP leadership paid income tax or had bank accounts, it responded "by stating that it did not have the mandate to gather such information". During proceedings, Brigadier Falak Naz was asked about the law that governs the mandate of the ISI, to which he responded that the ISI is governed by the 'laws of the country' but failed to mention any specific law. When the two-member bench asked the Attorney General to provide assistance regarding the law governing ISI and its mandate, the Attorney General "tendered a document (in a sealed envelope) which spelled out ISI's mandate, but requested that the mandate of ISI should not be disclosed". Paragraph 42 of the judgment further noted that the Attorney General "did not give any reason for such secrecy except that this was also the practice in other countries but did not cite the example of a single one". When the Supreme Court examined the precedent world over, it found that the United Kingdom, US, New Zealand, Australia, Canada and Norway have legislation governing their intelligence agencies and clearly delineating their mandates. Instead of clarifying the need to regulate the ISI, the prime minister chose to play the notification game with the chief of army staff".[6]

This new sectarian militant organization promoted interests of the Brelvi sect and gave courage to its leadership to challenge the Deobandi and Wahhabi influence in Pakistan. The Barelvi sect's leadership received election support from the TLP leadership. Pakistan Today (October 26, 2021) reported Tehrik-e-Labbaik Pakistan that put the capital under siege and held hostage the residents of the twin cities by its Faizabad dharna: "While the clerics blasted the civil and military leadership with their highly inflammable harangues, inciting their supporters to violence, there was no sign of the government moving against them. After the fall of the PML (N), the TLP was mainstreamed. It won three seats in the Sindh Assembly which boosted its morale. It rejected the Supreme Court ruling in Aasia Bibi's case and demanded that she may not be sent abroad. When the demand was rejected by the PTI government, the party initiated violent protests destroying public and private property. Pakistan Today noted on its editorial page.[7] Expert and analyst, Sushant Sareen in his research paper (Tehrik-E-Labbaik Pakistan: The New Face of Barelvi Activism. Occasional Paper No. 332, September 2021, Observer Research Foundation) noted some developments occurred in 1990s and emergence of Sunni Tehrik in Karachi. He also noted the resolve of ST to bring all Barelvis to a close and establish a strong political platform. The Tehreek Tahafuz Namoos-e-Risalat group organised street protests and mobilised people to target the Ahmadis and killed Salman Taseer, Governor of Punjab:

"In 07 November 2010, a session's court in Nankana Sahib in the Punjab province of Pakistan, sentenced to death a Christian woman, Aasia Bibi, on charges of committing blasphemy against the Prophet. Punjab Governor Salman Taseer met the woman in jail where he received her petition for mercy. He criticised the blasphemy law and said it only promoted extremism and quarrels between Islam and other religion.....The massive show of strength in Islamabad by the TLYRA shook the established religious parties, all of whom denounced the sit-in. The TLYRA announced 10 demands: imposing the Shariah; declaring Mumtaz Qadri a martyr and converting his jail cell into a national monument; banning anti-Islam NGOs; an assurance that the blasphemy law would not be changed; the unconditional release of all religious leaders and clerics, including those arrested or convicted on charges of terrorism and murder; removal of all Ahmediyyas and non- Muslims from government positions; and executing Aasia Bibi. After three days, the government and the TLYRA leaders agreed on a seven-point deal. While the government did not concede to anything substantial, the TLYRA managed to exhibit its clout. On the eve of the 2018 elections, most political analysts agreed that the TLP–the political party of TLYRA – was only going to play spoiler, especially for the then ruling party–PMLN. On its own, the TLP was expected to make little impact, despite its performance in some of the by-elections in the second half of 2017".[8]

Researcher on Strategic and Economic Affairs and Consultant with the National Security Council Secretariat (NSCS) Vaishali Basu Sharma in her recent analysis (Tehreek-e-Labbaik Pakistan: A Case of the Military Losing Control over Islamists-20 April 2021) has documented the role of Pakistan military in alliances making. Sharma also noted the hanging of Mumtaz Qadri and acquittal of Asia Bibi: "Given Nawaz Shareef's anti-military stance, the military establishment worked hard to make sure Imran Khan becomes the next Prime Minister in the 2018 general elections. To pressure the then ruling party PML-N, the military staked propping up the Tehreek-e-Labbaik, at that time considered a fringe pressure group. Suddenly the Tehreek-e-Labbaik appeared to be protesting everything from the hanging of Mumtaz Qadri to the acquittal of Asia Bibi. The run-up to 2018 elections witnessed attacks on political meetings, arrests of seasoned and likely-to-win politicians, censorship of the media and kidnapping of activists and journalists known to be critics of the military and, crucially, hardline right-wing parties entering the fray. The TLP's rapid rise in the political sphere of Pakistan was a direct outcome of the military establishment's tacit support to different religious groups in order to weaken the PMLN government. Throughout Pakistan's history, the establishment's policy of appeasing the religious groups has only encouraged their irrational demands. In November 2017, when the TLP organized a huge sit-in at Faizabad, demanding the sacking of Federal Law Minister Zahid Hamid over the "softening" of anti-blasphemy laws in the country".[9]

On 20 August 2021, The TLP was banned under the Anti-Terrorism Act. The party was seeking downgrade of Paris-Islamabad ties, among other demands. The PTI government presented a resolution on the expulsion of the French Ambassador to Pakistan in the National Assembly. Expert and analyst, PIA Krishnankutty in her commentary (All about Tehreek-e-Labbaik Pakistan, extremist group now outlawed by Imran Khan regime, the Print, 20 April, 2021) has highlighted the process of resolution that downgraded the France-Pakistan relationship. In her commentary, PIA Krishnankutty noted banning of the TLP under the Anti-Terrorism Act, 1997, while government continued to engage with TLP workers, who had been holding anti-France protests for more than a week after clashing with the police in Lahore: "However, before a vote could take place on the resolution, which could downgrade Paris-Islamabad ties, the speaker announced the formation of a special committee to discuss the matter and asked the government and the opposition to engage with each other to develop consensus on the issue. In a video statement, Pakistan's Interior Minister Sheikh Rashid said the decision to present the resolution was taken after a round of talks with the recently outlawed far-right political party, Tehreek-e-Labbaik Pakistan (TLP). The party was banned under the Anti-Terrorism Act, 1997. The government continued to engage with TLP workers, who had been holding anti-France protests for more than a week after clashing with the police in Lahore. Amid tensions, the French Embassy advised its citizens to leave the country temporarily. During the clashes, TLP workers took 11 policemen hostage. According to Rashid, 580 police personnel had sustained injuries and at least 30 cars had been destroyed during the violence. The captured policemen were later released after negotiations with the government. The TLP put forth four demands: the expulsion of the French ambassador over President Emmanuel Macron's backing of Prophet Muhammad caricatures last year; the release of party chief Saad Rizvi; removal of the ban on the party; and the release of party workers arrested as well as FIRs against them to be dropped"[10].

Analyst and expert, Sushant Sareen in his research paper (Tehrik-E-Labbaik Pakistan: The New Face of Barelvi Activism-Occasional Paper, 15 September 2021, Observer Research Foundation) has highlighted the killing of Salman Taseer and rally of Tehrik Tahaffuz-e-Khatm-e-Nabuwat celebrating his death and phenomenon of Mumtaz Qadri who killed the governor of Punjab. The rally demanded release of Qadri and built him up as a new Islamic hero. Mumtaz Qadri phenomenon was important not just because he killed a constitutional functionary but also because it was indicative of the potential of 'lone wolves' radicalised by extremist rhetoric and indoctrinated by Islamist preachers and politicians:

"On the day Taseer was killed, the Tehrik Tahaffuz-e-Khatm-e-Nabuwat held a rally celebrating his death, calling him "a Zionist agent". The next day, the religious parties declared their support for the assassin and blamed Taseer for getting killed. They also warned the government against repealing the blasphemy law. Lawyers of a district court in Islamabad showered flower petals on the assassin when he was produced in court. The Mumtaz Qadri phenomenon is important not just because he killed a constitutional functionary but also because it was indicative of the potential of 'lone wolves' radicalised by extremist rhetoric and indoctrinated by Islamist preachers and politicians. In Qadri's case, his mentor, according to first investigations, was a Barelvi cleric who taught him that Taseer was wajib-ul-Qatal (worthy of death) for speaking against the blasphemy law. Later it was found that Qadri was motivated by stories of how the first Caliph had treated a mercy petition from a woman punished for blasphemy and juxtaposed that with Taseer's sympathetic attitude towards Aasia Bibi, calling him a "Yazidi governor". The Islamists rallied for Qadri and demanded his release, building him up as a new Islamic hero. The case against him in court proceeded, regardless, and on 1 October 2011, an Anti-Terrorist Court (ATC) sentenced Mumtaz Qadri to death. Protests broke out across the country, and a bounty was placed on the head of the judge who sentenced Qadri, forcing him to leave the country. The ST, meanwhile, offered PKR 20 Crore as blood money to the family of Salman Taseer in exchange for Mumtaz Qadri's release. On 29 February 2016, Mumtaz Qadri was hanged, and violent protests broke out".[11]

However, on 20 September 2021, Dawn reported Interior Minister Sheikh Rashid Ahmed's resolve to resolve issues with Maulana Abdul Aziz through dialogue, as it wanted the situation in the capital to remain normal. Addressing a press conference in Islamabad, he said that there were several cases against Maulana Aziz but the government wanted the situation in the capital to remain normal. "That's why we keep talking to them," he said, adding that Maulana Aziz had an issue every other day. "Every day he has an issue and every day we try to resolve it," he said, adding that there were 511 madrassas and 1,000 mosques in the capital. "Out of 511, we have issues with only one, which we resolve through dialogue." Without naming the entity he was referring to, the minister said that the government had made such efforts with another religious organisation. "However, the result of that was not a good one,"he said. Moreover, journalist Umer Farooq in his article (For Pakistan's Security Establishment, Lal Masjid Is Not The Problem, Abdul Aziz knows how to attract Pakistan's media with emotional sloganeering and how to galvanize militant groups.[12] The Friday Times, 28 September 2021) has noted that for Pakistan's security establishment, Lal Masjid was not the problem, and is on the opinion that the white flag of the Taliban remained visible to all those who were visiting Melody Market and its adjacent bazaars:

"Maulana Abdul Aziz knows how to attract Pakistan's media with emotional sloganeering and knows how to galvanize the militant groups—the two elements needed to recreate July 2007-like situation in the city. For the media, he set the bait of cheap and emotional sloganeering, while for militants he put the bait of what they like most: blood. This time the white flag of the Afghan Taliban, which was hoisted on the roof of the red mosque, is the point of confrontation. The white flag of the Taliban remained visible to all those who were visiting the heart of the city—the Melody Market and its adjacent bazaars. For two weeks the police failed to force the mosque administration to remove the flags as they continued to demand the enforcement of Sharia law in the country in return for the removal of the flags. The flags were removed only after the federal government moved a contingent of riot police close to the mosque. The city administration, however, had placed barbed wires and concrete blocks around all the roads leading up to the mosque almost a year back. There are a large number of city residents who are fond of going to the Red Mosque for their Friday prayers. Therefore, the city administration did not prevent ordinary citizens from proceedings towards the mosque on Friday afternoon. "We have temporarily removed the flags on the condition that the city officials will put our demands before the government high ups and our demands are clear. We want the implementation of Sharia in the country on an immediate basis," said Shakeel Ghazi. There was a showdown between seminary students—who were assisted by armed members of militant groups—and Pakistani army commandos in July 2007 as a result of which more than around 100 students were killed in the army operation".[13]

Mullah Abdul Aziz of Red Mosque Islamabad in his recent interview with a local journalist (Quran orders to become terrorists: Maulana Abdul Aziz, SAMVADA-25 August 2021) communicated that the Holy Quran had ordained Muslims to become terrorists against enemies of Allah. His interview generated a new perception that now Pakistani sectarian clerics want to justify terrorism and jihad from the Holy Quran against non-Muslim states in Europe and Asia. His knowledge about the Holy Quran and Allah Almighty is shameful and deplorable but silence of all so called Muftis, religious scholars and political parties on his humiliation of the Holy Quran is under whelming. In his Tweet, Vivek Sinha raised the question of Pakistani Mullahs silence on Maulana Abdul Aziz remarks: "Maulana Abdul Aziz of Pakistan's Lal Masjid says clearly that Quran orders Muslims to become Terrorists. Is this is not Pakistani state-sponsored terrorism? He generated controversies about Allah Almighty and the Holy Quran, and clearly barricaded his stance on jihad against non-Muslim states.[14]

The Holy Quran never instructed or directed Muslims to become terrorists against the enemies of Allah Almighty. The Quran says: "When it is said to them: "Make no mischief on the earth," They say: "Why we only want to make peace. Of a surety, they are the ones who make mischief, but they realize (it) not". Al Baqara, 2:11).[15]" On 19 September 2021, a case was registered against Maulana Abdul Aziz in Islamabad for threatening policemen who came to remove Afghan Taliban's flags hoisted at Jamia Hafsa, a seminary run by the cleric's wife. Thus, Prime Minister Imran Khan's policy of appeasing radicals backfired while Lal Masjid Madrassa now openly inculcates young girls in the manner of beheading. Expert and analyst, Mrityunjoy Kumar Jha in his analysis (India Narrative, 09-12-2021) noted the exponentially growing trends of suicide terrorism and beheading in Pakistan: "Pakistan's notorious Lal Masjid is back in the news again. In a viral video, the young girl students were shown how to behead a person who disrespects Prophet Mohammad (PBU). In the background, the slogan of hardliner radical Tehreek-i-Labbaik Pakistan (TLP), "Gustakh-e-Rasool ki ek hi sazaa, Sartan se Juda, Sar tan se Juda" (Only one punishment for blasphemy against the prophet, separation of head from the body) was playing on the loudspeakers. It was the same slogan that supporters of TLP were chanting while they lynched and burnt the Sri Lankan factory manager Priyantha Kumara Diyawadana in Sialkot. Sharing the video clip, Pakistani journalist Gul Bukhari wrote on a Twitter post, "Students of Red Mosque Islamabad practicing how to behead a person accused of blasphemy. Pakistan's "kamyab jawan" (successful youth) project is proceeding rather well," a reference to the Pakistani Prime

Minister Imran Khan's project for youth of the country. Just three months back, the Pakistani Prime Minister Imran Khan had surrendered to the firebrand cleric Maulana Abdul Aziz and allowed them to hoist Taliban flags atop the infamous Lal Masjid, situated in the heart of the capital Islamabad. In a video, the head cleric of the Lal Masjid Maulana Abdul Aziz was seen with a Kalashnikov threatening the Pakistani forces of dire consequences if they removed those flags. "The Pakistan Taliban (TTP) will teach you all a lesson," he threatened them. The Islamic fundamentalist, Maulana Aziz had issued a "fatwa" that no one would attend the funerals of Pakistani soldiers and called for "agitations" against the government. As expected, Imran Khan had to surrender to him to keep the situation normal in the capital, which is already grabbing headlines after the New Zealand cricket team left the country without playing a single game, citing security concerns".[16]

The concept of suicide attacks, or dying in order to kill in the name of religion, becomes a supreme ideal of Taliban and Pakistani madrassas Mullahs. After the US invasion of Afghanistan, Taliban resorted to suicide terrorism to force the United States and its NATO allies to withdraw their forces from the country and restore Emirate Islami. Taliban and the IS-K became dominant forces in suicide terrorism to internationalize and justify it. Modern suicide terrorism emerged in Afghanistan after 9/11, but it was introduced in different shapes. Over the past two decades, the tactic of suicide terrorism in Afghanistan and Pakistan was modified and justified by religious clerics. Expert Assaf Moghadam (Suicide Terrorism, Occupation, and the Globalization of Martyrdom: A Critique of Dying to Win, published in 2006) has painted a true picture of that business in his paper: "the growing interest in suicide terrorism in recent years has generated a steep rise in the number of books that address a topic that is inherently fascinating—a mode of operations that requires the death of its perpetrator to ensure its success".[17]Analyst and writer, Florian Weig has noted (Afghanistan's Taliban: Legitimate Jihadists or Coercive Extremists?) that the Taliban wanted to introduce sharia and prohibit music and suppress women:

"The Taliban are usually depicted as ideological fighters–religious extremists who want to introduce harsh rules in Afghanistan, including the prohibition of music and the suppression of women. Their mode of governance stands in stark contrast to Western ideals.The fall of the Taliban government in 2001 was portrayed as a victory against terrorism and human rights abuses. However, the influence of the Taliban and other armed opposition groups is steadily growing again throughout Afghanistan. They describe themselves as 'jihadists' that fight against the government and its foreign supporters. According to a United States (US) Congress report, not even 60 percent of the country's districts were under Afghan government control or influence in 2017 (SIGAR 2017, 87). At the same time, the US was welcoming direct peace talks with the Taliban (Tolo News, February 24, 2016).[18] This development raises the question as to what the affected people–rather than the foreign interveners –think about the Taliban".

The Looting and ransacking of Afghanistan's natural resources by NATO and the United States, and their criminal militias suchlike the ISIS and Taliban terrorist groups, caused misunderstanding between the Afghans and International Coalition that they all were involved in looting of mineral resources of their country. The IS-K controlled parts of the country's rich mineral wealth, especially talc, chromite and marble. According to the Global Witness research report, several insurgents' groups, militias, Taliban and the ISIS were deeply involved in the plunder of these resources: "The Islamic State in Afghanistan (ISKP) controls major mining sites in eastern Afghanistan and has a strategic interest in the country's rich mineral resources, new Global Witness research shows–a powerful example of the wider threat posed by armed groups and corrupt actors in Afghan mining. The Islamic State in Afghanistan (ISKP) controls large talc, marble and chromite mines in the Islamic State stronghold of Achin district in the Nangarhar province of eastern Afghanistan–the same area where in April 2017 the US military dropped the 'Mother of All Bombs' against ISKP-held caves. Nangarhar was the deadliest Afghan province for US troops in 2017. An estimated 380, 000 tons of talc was imported into the United States in 2017. On average around 35 percent of US imports are from Pakistan, according to the US Geological Survey. From our research we also estimated that around 80 percent of Pakistan's 2016 exports of talc actually originated in Afghanistan. Of those exports, 42 percent went to the US, and another 36 percent went to EU countries, especially the Netherlands and Italy".[19]

The perception that Taliban are ideological fighter is totally wrong, the reason for that they are terrorists and act like terrorists, carrying out suicide attacks against civilians and destroying everything they don't like. They and the Pakistani ISI have committed war crimes, beheaded innocent Muslims, kidnapped women and children and used them for sexual exploitation. They are proxies of Pakistan's military establishment, barking for the

American Army and ISI equally. They have established suicide brigades, and threatened Afghanistan's neighbours. The Taliban's relationship with al Qaeda and the IS-K further generated fear and consternation. As Afghanistan remained a top destination for foreign terrorist groups, Taliban entered into alliances with different groups. The fall of Afghanistan to the Taliban generated a new terror threat in South and Central Asia. The Taliban's close relationship with several Pakistani terror groups and its inability to govern the whole country may turn Afghanistan into a nest of terror militias. In Afghanistan, close cooperation between Daesh and some disgruntled Taliban groups added to the pain of the Taliban Government. The Khorasan terrorist group, which emerged with a strong military power in 2015, is in control of important districts in Jalalabad province.

The group's military tactics included beheading, public prosecution, kidnapping, and torture, looting and raping, and also forcing families from their homes. Due to the weakness of Taliban and local administration, the IS-K expanded its networks to all districts of Jalalabad. Some of the groups including Quetta Shura, Tora Bora Jihadi group, Gul Buddin Hekmatyar group, Salafi group, Fidayee Karwan,Sia Pushan groups (identified as black-clad and masked terrorists) were in clandestine collaboration with the Khorasan group, TTP, and Lashkar-e-Islam group. In Mohmand Agency, Jamaat Al Ahrar and TTP were operating in collaboration with ISKP. Afghanistan is still run by proxy militias of different internal and external stakeholders. In October 2015, Kunduz was destroyed by these militias which looted banks, markets and houses. After the Soviet invasion of Afghanistan and emergence of Mujahedeen's militias in Pakistan and Iran, regional powers, US, NATO and the Arab world's military experts arrived in Pakistan to train, support, and arm every terrorist and extremist group to defeat the Soviet army in Afghanistan. All these private militias are still dancing to different tangos in all provinces of Afghanistan. They receive financial support from the different channels-challenged territorial authority of the country's national army. On 10 June 2022, Human Rights Watch reported Taliban's torture of civilians in Panjshir valley. "Since mid-May 2022, fighting has escalated in the province as National Resistance Front (NRF) forces have attacked Taliban units and checkpoints.[20]

The Taliban have responded by deploying to the province thousands of fighters, who have carried out search operations targeting communities. During search operations in other provinces, Taliban forces committed summary executions and enforced disappearances of captured fighters and other detainees, which are war crimes. Taliban forces in Panjshir province quickly resorted to beating civilians in their response to fighting against the opposition National Resistance Front," said Patricia Gossman, associate Asia Director at Human Rights Watch. "The Taliban's longstanding failure to punish those responsible for serious abuses in their ranks put more civilians at risk." Human Rights Watch noted. Afghanistan's ruling Taliban illegally detained and tortured residents in northern Panjshir province for their alleged links to armed opposition forces, Human Rights Watch reported. "Taliban forces in Panjshir province have quickly resorted to beating civilians in their response to fighting against the opposition National Resistance Front," said Patricia Gossma, the associate Asia director at Human Rights Watch. "The Taliban's longstanding failure to punish those responsible for serious abuses in their ranks puts more civilians at risk," she added in the statement. However, Human Rights Watch on 07 July 2022, in its report noted: "Taliban security forces have summarily executed and forcibly disappeared alleged members and supporters of an Islamic State offshoot in eastern Afghanistan, Human Rights Watch said. Since the Taliban took power in August 2021, residents of Nangarhar and Kunar provinces east of Kabul have discovered the bodies of more than 100 men dumped in canals and other locations.[21]

Chapter 2

The Army, Agencies and Political Alliances

On 12 May 2022, Muslim League leader, Maryam Nawaz warned that the army chief must have a flawless image. She criticized former Chief of ISI Faiz Hameed for his political role in orchestrating her conviction in a corruption case. Maryam Nawaz also hammered the Pakistan army for genocide in Baluchistan. Balochs were suppressed, killed and subjected to enforced disappearance by the ISI and the army, that being the case, ISI and the Army lost public confidence due to their political role, and corruption. Their loyalty to the state is in question. People, an important constituent of the elements that define a State, are fast losing faith in their military and intelligence institutions. The point is, the Inter-Service Intelligence (ISI) lacks adequate intelligence information collection experience from remote areas of Balochistan, Sindh and Waziristan, the agency lacks trained manpower, fails to understand modern technology, it lacks proper intelligence sharing approach with policymakers and lacks technic of actionable intelligence. On 19 October 2021, News-18, in its news report, noted that Imran Khan and Qamar Javed Bajwa were boiling over the new ISI chief:

"The overriding clout that the army enjoys in Pakistan is well known with the country's civilian rulers widely seen as being beholden to its military establishment. Which would explain why an impasse between Pakistan Prime Minister Imran Khan and its army chief Gen. Qamar Javed Bajwa over the appointment of the new chief of the powerful Inter-Services Intelligence (ISI) has raised eyebrows and made the ruling classes in Pakistan uncomfortable? Reports seeking to explain PM Khan's evident reluctance to sign off on the appointments have pointed to the suggestion that they were made unilaterally by Bajwa and that Khan wanted Hameed to continue in the post for at least till the winter was over, given that the situation in Afghanistan remains volatile in the wake of the Taliban's return to power in the neighbouring country. Hameed had, in fact, made an appearance in Kabul as the Taliban top rung was working on forming the interim government in Afghanistan with observers saying that clearly pointed to the ISI's deep involvement with the Islamists. Close ties between Khan and Hameed have also been cited as a possible reason why the Pakistan PM has held off on endorsing the appointments made by Bajwa, who is said to have told Khan that he could not expect the incumbent to be "retained forever". News-18 reported.[1]

Newspaper Dawn reported (Rare consensus among rivals on ISI's role in civilian setup-June 4, 2022) concordance of PML-N and PTI—that the country's premier spy agency, the Inter-Services Intelligence (ISI), should be under civilian control and answerable to the parliament after the PML-N-led coalition government gave the agency legal cover to screen civilian officials. PML-N leader and former Information Minister Pervaiz Rasheed said on Twitter that if the ISI was being tasked with vetting civilian officials, then the spy agency should be placed under civilian control and be answerable to parliament. Former information Minister and PTI leader Fawad Chaudhry agreed with Rasheed and said that if "institutions wanted to increase their role in civilian affairs, and then they would have to pay for it in the form of public accountability". "The institution (ISI) has to think about what role it wants to play in Pakistan's politics· A discussion is needed on the new roles of civil institutions and institutions after the media revolution," he tweeted. Meanwhile, former Senate chairman, PPP's Raza Rabbani termed the decision to task ISI with screening civil servants "surprising", saying it amounted to "ceding civilian space". Dawn reported.[3] Moreover, Outlook Magazine of India in its report (Pakistan Government Formally Assigns Govt Officials' Screening to Spy Agency ISI: Report Outlook India, 07 August 2022) noted clearance of Bureaucrats promotion by the ISI agency:

"Pakistan's premier spy agency ISI had always informally screened and verified the country's civil servants, but Prime Minister Shehbaz Sharif has now officially tasked the Inter-Services Intelligence (ISI) with the job, providing a legal cover and formalizing a job that the agency had been doing for a long time, as per a media report. The Dawn newspaper reported that Sharif had notified the DG ISI as the Special Vetting Agency (SVA) for verification and screening of all Public Office Holders (Officers Category), according to the Establishment Division notification in exercise of powers conferred on the Prime Minister. The quoted laws empower the prime minister to amend or make rules for the civil bureaucracy. The direction was issued from the office of the Prime Minister on May 6. By doing so, Sharif has given legal cover to a practice that had already been in place but had not been formalized as part of the protocol, as per the Dawn report. A senior official from the Establishment Division told Dawn on the condition of anonymity that the ISI and the Intelligence Bureau (IB) both send their reports about civil servants before they are posted on important assignments. Reports are especially sent to the Central Selection Board (CSB) at the time of promotion of bureaucrats. According to the official, notwithstanding the notification, the IB will continue to send its reports as per routine. The official said that since the government has now given legal effect to reports issued by the ISI, these could henceforth be used in courts as valid legal documents, the newspaper said. However, a former Establishment Division Secretary disagreed. He noted that though the prime minister has the power to amend or make rules for the bureaucracy, it would have been better if the Establishment Division would have issued a Statutory Regulatory Order (SRO) to amend the Appointments, Promotions and Transfer (APT) Rules governing the civil bureaucracy if it wanted to give the ISI formal charge of the vetting process".[4]

The ISI's role in Pakistani politics is of great importance and is controversial as well. Appointment on top government posts and reports about their family and political background is also prepared by the ISI agency. That is why the involvement of the military establishment in politics has paved the way for ISI involvement in politics and government. Senior Fellow in IDSA, Dr. Bidanda M. Chengappa in an article (The ISI Role in Pakistan's Politics), has reviewed the involvement of ISI in Pakistan's politics and its intransigence to relinquish its political role in making political alliances: "The Inter-Services Intelligence (ISI) Directorate has over five decades of nationhood emerged into a powerful institution in Pakistan. It has been active as an organisation both under military rule and civilian regimes. The ISI gains importance from the fact that the political and military leaderships have always perceived threats to their national security since independence. The role of an intelligence agency is to serve as the first line of defence by providing the government with advance information about threats to national security. The ISI has a monolithic organisational structure which oversees both external and internal intelligence operations in the country. The organisation's internal intelligence operations tend to be generally associated with the abuse of power. This negative view needs to be linked to whether or not the government has clearly defined their charter of duties for internal operations. Pakistan, like other countries, has serious problems in managing its intelligence agencies. This is evident from the fact that in over five decades of nationhood there have been six committees to review their functioning. To complicate matters, the country has experienced 24 years of military rule in 52 years of nationhood, which enables greater scope for misuse of intelligence agencies".[5]

After a long political journey, the ISI became a constant need of every political party dancing on the political theatre in Pakistan the reason for that ISI has been making alliances and dissolving parliaments since the 1980s. The agency is being sponsoring terrorism and intelligence war since 1990s. Its influence on security and foreign policy formulation process and its use of terrorist groups against neighbouring states to destabilize the region is an under whelming development. The ISI personnel are being used as an instrument to impede the development of trade ties between India, Afghanistan and India. The ISI has a close relationship with the Taliban, Harkat ul Ansar and the Lashkar-e-Toiba, which are extremely active in waging terrorist operations against neighbouring states. Senior Fellow in IDSA, Dr. Bidanda M. Chengappa in an article (The ISI Role in Pakistan's Politics) has highlighted the ISI role in dissolving parliament and governments, and political loyalties of ISI chiefs in 1980s and 1990s:

"The ISI in September 1988, headed by Lt General Hamid Gul cobbled together the Opposition parties in Pakistan and formed the IJI in order to defeat the Benazir Bhutto-led PPP from coming to power. Clearly, caretaker President Ghulam Ishaq Khan and the COAS General Beg were not keen on Benazir winning the elections and they used all the resources at their command namely the ISI, the MI, the IB and the police special branches to thwart her political victory. Former Prime Minister Benazir Bhutto was "in office but out of power" as she was compelled to adhere to certain conditions of the military leadership in order to assume office. These conditions included: (a) to continue the late General Zia's Afghan policy (b) allow General Mirza Aslam Beg and Lt General Hamid Gul to continue in their appointments as Chief of Army Staff and Director General ISI respectively (c) not to depress the defence budget (d) not to initiate any accountability proceedings against army personnel. After Benazir became the Prime Minister she had a problem with the ISI in the sense that an agency which was working against her till the other day now formed part of her government. She associated the agency with her father's judicial execution and saw it as a repressive arm of the military which therefore amounted to an attitudinal problem towards the ISI. In tune with this mind-set one of her first moves was to sack Brigadier (retd) Imtiaz from the ISI and close down its political division in early 1989. She appointed Major (retd) Masood Sharif, a close friend of her husband, Asif

Zardari as the Director IB. Benazir had serious differences with the ISI over its Afghan policy in early 1989 and this resulted in a rift between the PM and the ISI leadership".[6]

In the aftermath of the terrorist attacks in Punjab and Sindh, the ISI became subject to a hot-blooded assessment. The IB (Pakistan) and ISI suffered from lack of check and balance, and the influence of government and private stakeholders. In Punjab and Khyber Pakhtunkhawa, the ISI and civilian intelligence supported sectarian groups. Shortfall of scientific collaboration and interoperability between the ISI and civilian agencies, and intelligence agencies of neighbouring states prompted misunderstanding about the credibility of the ISI. The ISI and civilian agencies have been accused of shameless inability and inefficiency in handling the tottering state, particularly over the past four decades. They have been deeply involved in massive corruption cases since 1971. Pakistan is, moreover, at war with itself. This partial civil war has been caused by the misadventures of many state agencies, as well as of many internal and external forces. In 2018, General Qamar Bajwa established terrorist units in all EU Pakistani Embassies in order to kill anti-establishment writers, bloggers and journalist, but in 2020, His plan was uncovered by a British Pakistani Gohir Khan.

On 25 January 2022, Dawn newspaper reported (Hitman grilled in blogger Ahmad Waqas Goraya's murder plot case, Atika Rehnab) the trial of a British Pakistani Gohir Khan who travelled to the Netherlands to kill the journalist and blogger Ahmad Waqass Goraya but was arrested in Britain. Alison Morgan QC led the prosecution, and questioned why Mr Khan did not approach the police when he was contacted by the ISI middleman Muzamil to kill someone; why Mr Khan kept asking if the 'job' or killing was a debt-related one; why he purchased a knife; and why he made efforts to deceive the immigration authorities to enter the Netherlands. While maintaining that he was not guilty of intent to kill, the defendant claimed he "never intended to kill anyone", but that he "wanted to get money out of Muzamil as he owed him money". He said he purchased the knife to cut steak, fruit and bread and travelled to the Netherlands to convince Muzamil to give him more money. Dawn reported.[7] However, on 29 January 2022, Friday Times reported the British-Pakistani man, Gohir Khan, who was declared guilty by a UK court for his involvement in a plot to kill self-exiled blogger Ahmad Waqass Goraya in the Netherlands. BBC reported that the jury issued its verdict two days after the trial was concluded in London following completion of both sides' arguments. During the hearings, the prosecution maintained that Gohir Khan had travelled to Rotterdam in the Netherlands with the intention to kill Goraya and that he had a tool using which he was going to commit the crime. He was reportedly going to be rewarded heavily by the Inter-Services Intelligence (ISI) for his action, with a payment of £100,000.[8]

According to Mrityunjoy Kumar Jha (16-01-2022) that Pakistan's notorious spy agency Inter-Services Intelligence (ISI) hired Mr. Khan to kill journalist Waqas Goraya. The trial court charged a hitman, accusing him of plotting. "According to the prosecution, the notorious Pakistani spy agency, ISI contacted London based Muhammad Gohir Khan, a British citizen of Pakistani origin through a middleman and offered to £100000 to kill Goraya who has been living in Rotterdam, Netherlands since he fled Pakistan after receiving death threats. Shamelessly the ISI and Muhammad Gohir Khan exchanged 2000 text messages which authenticated incompetency and a weak approach of ISI to intelligence operations. Khan reported to his Pakistan based ISI handler Muzammil (Mudz) and asked for more information on the target. Both of them started arguing over money when it became clear to Khan that he could not spot the target and Mudz was backtracking from transferring £10,000 immediately to cover expenses. "ISI has long been using abductions and killings to silence anyone who dares to question and expose their actions. In 2019, Pakistani blogger and journalist Bilal Khan, known for criticising the country's powerful military and the spy agency ISI was hacked to death allegedly by the ISI. However, journalist Hamid Mir of Geo TV, was taken off the air and threatened after he named the Pakistani military for targeting journalists".[9] Consequently, a British-Pakistani Gohir Khan was jailed for life imprisonment for conspiring to kill Netherlands-based, self-exiled blogger and activist Ahmad Waqass Goraya. Now the question is how the so called number one Pakistani intelligence agency will show its transmogrified face to the public when it exchanged 2000 text messages with the killer.

World News (17 February 2022) reported the ISI and General Bajwa game who has already established a terrorist and killer squad in Pakistan's High Commission in London to target critics, political activists and journalists: "In turn, it has led to a reopening of enquiries into the death of Karima Baloch, campaigner for an independent Balochistan, whose body was found in a lake in Canada in December 2020. Threats to her life back in Pakistan had forced Baloch to flee to Canada in 2015, where she was given political asylum. From Canada, Baloch continued her fight for Baluchistan's independence, and paid for that fight with her life.

In addition to the Netherlands, the UK and Canada, threats to the lives of Pakistani political exiles are also being investigated in France, where a journalist has encountered danger to his life. In one case, Yunas Khan was told by the French police that Prime Minister Imran Khan's ruling party, Tehreek-e-Insaf, was behind a conspiracy to get rid of the journalist. Contrary to conventional wisdom, exposure from investigations into a slew of assassination conspiracies may be beneficial publicity for Pakistani intelligence in circles that are willing to invest in political assassinations worldwide. The recent plots against dissidents on the continent, brought to light by several investigations, could point to a new policy taking shape under the watchful eyes of the intelligence agency where the void left by the old regimes in Libya, Iraq, and others is sought to be filled by Pakistan".[10]

The involvement of the army and ISI in politics, and their collaboration with extremist and terrorist organizations in India and Afghanistan has caused consternation, state collapse, torture and international isolation. The shameless and audacious role of the army and ISI in toppling the Imran Khan government further became suspicious in the eyes of civil society and politicians. On 12 June 2022 the Guardian reported Pakistani politicians and activists raised fears about the military increasing its control over the country's public life after Prime Minister Shehbaz Sharif, gave the ISI spy agency vetting power over civil service appointments: "It is widely perceived in Pakistan that politicians need the military's backing to come to power, but many now fear that bureaucrats could also need the same support for their appointment and postings. "If we keep in mind Pakistan's history of takeovers and the sway that military has over our politics, this decision will weaken civil bureaucracy and compromise their independence," said Senator Mustafa Nawaz Khokhar. "We have shot ourselves in the foot and it's a decision worth reconsidering." Raza Rabbani, the former chair of the senate, called Sharif's decision an attack on the constitution. "The concept of civilian supremacy is tarnishing," he said.[11]

On 05 June 2022, The Week Magazine's Web Desk (Pakistan: Demand to hold ISI accountable unites political rivals: Agency has been authorised to screen public officials) in its comment on Pakistani politics noted civilian resentment towards the army and the ISI: "Pakistani politics, while always polarized, arguably became more toxic since Imran Khan became prime minister in 2018. And the bickering has increased since Imran was forced to step down in April. However, there was a rare show of consensus among the warring political parties on a contentious issue: Need for the ISI to be held accountable. The ISI (Inter-Services Intelligence) is Pakistan's intelligence agency and is part of the military apparatus. While notorious in India and the West for its links to terrorists, the ISI has also been planned for its influence in Pakistani politics and government. The agency is not accountable to the civilian government. On June 2, the Shehbaz Sharif government issued a notification that authorised the ISI to act as 'special vetting agency' for verifying and screening public officials before they take up important positions. The Magazine noted.[12]

The Human Rights Commission of Pakistan also expressed concern over the Prime Minister's decision. "Even if this practice was already in place, it goes against democratic norms," it said. "The role of the military in civilian affairs needs to recede if Pakistan is to move forward as a democracy." The Newspaper reported. The ISI (Inter-Services Intelligence) is notorious in India and the West for its links to terrorists. Geo TV News reported: "decision of the government to screen people before their appointment, posting or promotion to high posts aims at improving the performance of the government and ensuring transparency among bureaucrats and other public office holders, who are often accused of malpractices for personal gains". On 05 July 2022, the Hindu newspaper reported Chief of Pakistan's spy agency ISI strict orders to all commanders to stay away from politics following directives from Army chief Gen. Qamar Javed Bajwa to offset a smear campaign against the military by ousted Prime Minister Imran Khan's party.[13]

Lieutenant General Nadeem Anjum, Director General (DG) of Pakistan's Inter-Services Intelligence (ISI), personally issued the instructions to his subordinates, The Express Tribune newspaper reported. The spymaster further said that there would be zero-tolerance for violations and any intelligence official found violating the directives would have no place in the premier agency. Pakistan's largest political parties including in government and opposition PML-N and PTI agreed that the country's spy agency, the Inter-Services Intelligence (ISI), should be under civilian control and answerable to the Parliament. Pakistan's ruling alliance questioned Prime Minister Shehbaz Sharif's decision to empower the spy agency, Inter-Services Intelligence (ISI) to conduct verification of all government officers. All these forces are working on divergent agendas, with little care about the future of Pakistani citizens and the implications of these deadly agendas for South Asia and the rest of the world. The war in neighbouring Afghanistan is weakening Pakistan as a modern state. The longer the war in Afghanistan continues, the more it will complicate the situation in Pakistan.

In view of this illegal business, the ISI lost its professional capabilities and hung in the air as a militant agency. Rivalry between the IB and ISI boiled over in June 2017 when a Joint Investigation Team (JIT) probing alleged money laundering by the Sharif family made a written complaint to the Supreme Court that the IB was wiretapping JIT members, including ISI and military intelligence personnel. The JIT further reported that the IB was hampering its inquiries, adding that military-led intelligence agencies were not on "good terms" with the IB. It said that IB had collected intelligence on members of the JIT from the National Database and Registration Authority (NADRA) and presented it to Prime Minister Nawaz Sharif for use against them. In the present situation, it is not clear what roles are being allocated to the three major agencies.

The crucial question that needs to be addressed is whether these agencies function under the watchful eyes of an elected government or are they still so sturdy that they are instrumental in installing or toppling such governments. All civilian and military agencies have a specific mind set, their sectarian affiliation and dearth of electronically trained manpower, lack of professional surveillance approach, and the absence of a proper intelligence sharing culture, raised serious questions about their credibility. Pakistan's military establishment and its secret agencies have been using jihadists in Afghanistan to achieve their strategic goal. Pakistan's backed Taliban's terrorist regime fighting to control natural resources and sites in different provinces of Afghanistan. It was reported in May 2019 that illegal mining of gold and other precious minerals dramatically increased in Taliban-controlled regions close to the border with Pakistan. Intelligence community of Pakistan faces numerous challenges, including a widespread lack of political support, public confidence, corruption, sectarian affiliations, political and ethnic associations.

The ISI and civilian intelligence agencies have ultimately failed to bring Gallus-Gallus from the remote regions of Sindh, Khyber Pakhtunkhwa and Balochistan provinces due to their inability to balloon out their networks to these regions and make a friendly relationship with the local population. General Faiz Hameed, former DG of ISI visited Kabul in 2021 to finalize the Taliban cabinet. Inter-Services Intelligence (ISI) forced the Taliban to announce an interim government that was guaranteed to preserve ISI's control over the crankshaft of power in Kabul. The ISI also secretly announced a coalition of small jihadist groups (The Islamic Invitation Alliance) in Afghanistan, which was separated from the Taliban and the ISKP. The purpose of the formation of this alliance was to crush Taliban leadership if they refused to follow the ISI's instructions. Foreign Policy Magazine reported the Islamic Invitation Alliance (IIA) was founded in 2020 with funding from the ISI and had been on the radar of US intelligence for more than a year. General Faiz Hameed's interference in Afghanistan and the constitution of a controversial cabinet there caused his removal by the Army Chief General Bajwa.

Chapter 3

How and why Tablighi Jamaat become a Major Intelligence Infrastructure of International Political and Military Stakeholders?

One of the largest Islamic extremist intelligence networks of contemporary times, in terms of both geographical spread and number of activists, the Tablighi Jamaat has received attention of states where it operates with different intelligence shapes, strategies and recruitment plans. Tablighi Jamaat, a South Asian Deobandi-Barelvi organization that played an ambiguous role in India and Pakistan, spied for some states, trained and recruited Muslims and Christians, and established intelligence networks in more than 100 European, Asian and African countries. With increasing frequency, terrorist plots in the West uncovered Tablighi Jamaat's linkages. A unit of Aadhyaasi Media and Content Services Private Limited, OpIndia it its news commentary (Tablighi Jamaat and its links to terrorist organizations: History of association to Al Qaeda, Taliban and Kashmiri terrorists: Secret US documents released by WikiLeaks in 2011 revealed that some Al Qaeda operatives used the Jamaat to get visas and fund their travel to Pakistan. They also lived in and around Delhi, the documents said- 31 March, 2020) noted the role of Tablighi Jamaat in spreading CIVID-19 in India, and its relations with Al Qaeda terrorist group:

"The role of Tablighi Jamaat in the spreading of the Wuhan Coronavirus across numerous states of India has come to light. At least ten people have died thus far after attending an Islamic religious event organized by the Islamic missionary organization in Markaz, Nizamuddin at the national capital. India is not the only country affected by the recklessness of the Tablighi Jamaat. Other South Asian countries are bearing the brunt of it as well. Under such circumstances, the Tablighi Jamaat's links with terrorist organizations such as Al Qaeda become hugely significant. Secret US documents released by WikiLeaks in 2011 revealed that some Al Qaeda operatives used the Jamaat to get visas and fund their travel to Pakistan.

They also lived in and around Delhi, the documents said. Referring to Saudi Arabia national Abdul Bukhary, as "a veteran jihadist", the report prepared by US authorities in-charge of Guantanamo Bay in Cuba, said a Jamaat member, whom he met in 1985-1986 helped to procure his visa for Pakistan. "One of the JT (Jamaat Tablighi) members procured detainee's visa for Pakistan, after which detainee and another Saudi travelled to Lahore," the report prepared on July 25, 2007 said. "While in New Delhi, detainee was introduced to the leader of the JT and asked to make a life commitment to the organisation. Detainee told JT that he needed to think about it because he did not want to commit his life to servitude, pilgrimage, and missionary work. Detainee returned to Lahore for two weeks and then travelled to Saudi Arabia," the document revealed by WikiLeaks said."[1]

The Tablighi Jamaat is also facilitating extremism and terrorism in South Asia and Europe, and recruits Muslims and Christians to balloon out its infrastructure. Harkat-ul-Mujahedeen, the Taliban and al Qaeda are being facilitated in Afghanistan and Pakistan by Tablighi Jamaat. Once a facilitator identifies such candidates, he often will segregate them from the main congregation in the mosque or community center and put them into small prayer circles or study groups where they can be more easily exposed to jihadist ideology, Stratfor noted. The 07 July 2005, London bombings were facilitated (Mohammed Siddique Khan and Shahzad Tanweer) by Tablighi Jamaat. "After Khan and Tanweer left the Tablighi mosque, they began attending the smaller Iqra Learning Center bookstore in Beeston, where they reportedly were exposed to frequent political discussions about places such as Iraq, Kashmir and Chechnya". Stratfor noted.[2]

Experts and analysts, Fred Burton and Scott Stewart in their report (Tablighi Jamaat: An Indirect Line to Terrorism-The Stratfor January 23, 2008) highlighted terror links of Tablighi Jamaat in Europe, US and Asia: "Like Khan and Tanweer, many jihadists desire to travel to Pakistan for training, while others want to get to Afghanistan, Kashmir or other places to fight jihad. However, the travel environment is far different today than it was in the early 1980s, when 747 jetliners packed with jihadists from Saudi Arabia and other places flew into Pakistan enroute to fight the Soviets in Afghanistan. Foreigners travelling to Pakistan today cannot enter the country without a visa, and Pakistani authorities are no longer inclined to issue visas to jihadists, as Jeffrey Battle and the other members of the Portland Seven had to learn the hard way. Shortly after the U.S. invasion of Afghanistan, the friends travelled to China with the intention of entering Afghanistan by way of Pakistan. Once at the Chinese-Pakistani border, however, they found they could not enter Pakistan without a visa. After spending a frustrating month trying to obtain visas from the Pakistani Embassy in Beijing, the seven aspiring jihadists decided to go their separate ways. Battle, who reportedly once served as a bodyguard for Black Panther leader Quanell X, later attempted to obtain a visa to Pakistan by saying he was affiliated with TJ. The Pakistanis, probably recognizing him from his prior (and apparently somewhat vocal) visa attempts, denied him again, though he was able to get a visa to travel to Bangladesh using the feigned connection to TJ. Unable to make his way from Bangladesh to Pakistan or Afghanistan, however, Battle returned to the United States, where he was later arrested. He was sentenced to 18 years in prison after pleading guilty to charges of seditious conspiracy and waging war against the United States.[3]

The mode adopted by Tablighi Jamaat is to facilitate terrorist groups in Europe and Africa. Tablighi Jamaat remained out of the limelight due to its unorganised structure and missionary nature, but after the US invasion of Afghanistan, it became clear that the group was involved in recruitment of EU Muslims and Christians. Tablighi Jamaat aided Al Qaeda members in getting visas and funds to travel from Pakistan. Moreover, several other cases from Kenya, Somalia and Pakistan make it amply clear that Tablighi Jamaat is used as an acceptable conduit by Islamic terrorist organisations to facilitate travels of their members. The Tablighi Jamaat supported Siddique Khan and his group members in London attacks. A Deobandi Islamic scholar, Maulana Muhammad Ilyas established Tablighi Jamaat in 1926 in India. National Security Adviser and a former Director General of Intelligence Bureau (IB) of India, Mr. Ajit Doval argued: "The movement was never viewed adversely by the government." But the Tablighi Jamaat has been banned in some Central Asian countries such as Uzbekistan, Tajikistan and Kazakhstan, whose governments see its puritanical preaching as extremist". Expert and analyst, Arsalan Khan in his recent research paper (Contested Sovereignty: Islamic Piety, Blasphemy politics and the paradox of Islamization in Pakistan-08 Jun 2022), explained the rise of a range of Islamic forces in Pakistan and the role of Tablighi Jamaat in popularizing Blasphemy:

"Pakistan has witnessed the rise of a range of Islamic forces that claim to be defending Islam from what they imagine to be a deluge of incidents of blasphemy, a veritable moral panic organized around a set of blasphemy laws pertaining to the regulation and protection of Islam. The violence of blasphemy politics, which is disproportionately directed at sectarian and religious minorities, is predicated on the claim that is the duty and mandate of the state to enforce the blasphemy laws, and where the state fails, the onus falls on ordinary Muslims to fulfil the demands of Islam. In this article, I focus on the response to this blasphemy politics by Pakistani Tablighis, practitioners of the transnational Islamic piety movement the Tablighi Jamaat. Like other Islamic groups in Pakistan, Tablighis consider blasphemy to be a grave sin and a deep threat to the Islamic community, but Tablighis believe that the solution to the growing incidence of blasphemy is to spread virtue through their distinct form of face-to-face preaching (dawat).[4]" South Asia Democratic Forum in its research paper (Policy Brief 10–Tablighi Jamaat and its role in the Global Jihad. South Asia Democratic Forum 11 December 2020) has noted some aspects of extremist and intelligence training of the Tablighi Jamaat in Europe and Asia:

"In spite of this, up until this point, the majority of critical evaluations by international intelligence have not reached public discourse or political decision-making processes in the states where TJ holds a significant presence. Especially in Europe and the US, TJ remains largely unknown outside Muslim communities – and when known, actions and motives are misread. This lack of knowledge regarding the dissemination of an Islamic supremacist agenda facilitates TJ's function as a driving force for Islamic extremism and as a major recruiting agency for the cause of Global Jihad - the movement bluntly threatens societies based on liberal and democratic norms. TJ has a relatively clandestine character, but reports point to TJ being extremely effective at spreading Islamic fundamentalism. In sum, TJ is seen as an essential component of a phenomenon which the French political- sociologist Bernard Rougier (2020) calls an 'Islamist Ecosystem'. We believe this concept is most useful to understand the role that TJ plays in the Global Jihad. It appears that there is a growing awareness within Germany's intelligence community regarding potential causal links between TJ's missionary activities, particularly religious training and instruction courses, and the radicalisation of individual followers. The BfV warned already in 2005 that 'trainings by TJ can constitute for individual young Muslims an entry into Islamism and – subsequently – also into Islamist-terrorist groups'23 (BMI, 2006, p.194). The federal agency emphasizes the significance of study tours abroad [namely those to Pakistan] offered by TJ. It is stated that 'successfully proselytised people are often provided several months of training events in Pakistani Qur'anic schools [madrasas]. Such intensive training courses can indoctrinate participants and make them receptive to Islamist ideas'24 (BMI 2006, p.226). 'In individual cases, trainees then found their way to "Mujahedeen" training camps in Afghanistan (BMI 2006, p.226)".[6]

Unquestionably, Pakistani intelligence agencies and military establishment are in full control of the Tablighi Jamaat's Intelligence Infrastructure, recruiting their educated young preachers in their intelligence centres and then task them to collect political, economic, military and technological intelligence information from across the globe. In its annual congregation and gathering in Raiwand, Lahore Pakistan, expert of intelligence, terrorism, extremism, military generals, bureaucrats, political and religious scholars, member of worldwide intelligence agencies, weapons experts, and technology experts participate to share their expertise with each other, designing worldwide strategies, planning jihad and financially sponsoring of Terrorism. Pakistan army and its intelligence agencies organize suchlike gathering every year and invite military and intelligence experts from Middle East, South Asia, Central Asia, Europe and Africa to their centres and recruit them to further Pakistan's Jihadist agenda. All participants retrieve new instructions, new programs, new guidance and return to their countries to undertake new jihadist programs. Pakistan's retired military generals and officers lead different groups in different states to further Pakistan's foreign policy objectives through the platform of Tablighi Jamaat.

Political, religious and military bureaucracy of the Tablighi Jamaat is consisted of retired military generals, retired bureaucrats and intellectuals. They have established separate military and intelligence commands for Europe, South Asia, Central Asia and SouthEast Asia in order to establish contacts with intellectuals, government officials and intelligence stakeholders. The leadership train their agents in their intelligence schools. They are being sent to war zones in Europe and Asia. Several European intelligence agencies have prepared intelligence reports and papers about the clandestine activities of the Tablighi Jamaat, and its secret recruitment programme for Muslims and converted Christians. The groups have been recruiting and converting men and women for its extremist and intelligence networks in Europe since years, while European intelligence agencies missed the boat and recently recognised the other side of the mirror.

Members of Tablighi Jamaat are actively in contact with the local population, building mosques, preaching centres, intelligence recruitment centres and collecting millions in EU currency to further expand its extremist and terrorist operations to Africa and Middle East. This author is witness to many faces of the Tablighi intelligence networks by visiting their centres times and again. Radicalization always emerges in specific places, and these places significantly shape the way people engage or disengage with extremist activities. The French authorities focus predominantly on Islamist radicalisation and jihadism, even though violent extremism is not bound by a certain ideology and neither is radicalisation. The government submitted, in December 2020, a bill to the parliamentarians with the purpose of tackling radicalisation. South Asia Democratic Forum in its research paper (Policy Brief 10–Tablighi Jamaat and its role in the Global Jihad. By South Asia Democratic Forum-11 December 2020), has uncovered an investigation undertaken by EU intelligence agencies against the illegal activities of Tablighi Jamaat:

"The French intelligence agency Direction Générale de la Sécurité Intérieure (DGSI, General Directorate for Internal Security) in its 2018 report (state of the situation regarding the lodging of Islamic fundamentalism in France) described TJ28 as one of the four most active Islamist movements in the country–besides the Frères Musulmans (Muslim Brotherhood), Salafists (Salafists), and the Mouvement Turc (Turkish Movement)–constituting 'the ultimate risk' in the form of 'an advent of a counter-society on national territory' (DGSI, 2018, p.3). The DGSI is particularly vigilant regarding TJ's growing influence within the educational system. More specific concerns regard the indoctrination of the teenager and parents by TJ supervisors, the influence of TJ imams on children education, and the immense difficulties faced by non-Muslim families (foremost Jewish ones) to get their children enrolled in public educational institutions where the majority of children are Muslims (DGSI, 2018, pp.62-63). This partly reflects the threat potential of antisemitism among Tablighi identified by German intelligence agencies. Another major concern of the DGSI is that through to the strong cohesion among active Tablighi–reinforced through religious practises, teaching missions, and omnipresent prayers among others–the social ties of adherents outside the Tablighi community disappear quickly (DGSI, 2018, p.108). Indeed, many Tablighi are experiencing a 'turn-over' within the movement. Here the DGSI states that 'in general, after observing an important rigorism in his practice of Islam, the individual ends up moving away from the movement. The weakness of the religious discourse served in the organisation (based on some literalist precepts) and the lack of prospects offered by the preaching activity have the effect of causing individuals to leave to other Islamist 'offers', especially Salafists' (DGSI, 2018, p.108)".[6]

European intelligence agencies have established several surveillance units to closely watch terrorist and secret business of Tablighi Jamaat in towns and cities. Italian and Brussels intelligence agencies have become vigilant to prevent radicalization and extremist activities of Tablighi Jamaat, while German BND supports other members and experts of the European intelligence community to adopt professional measures in controlling the illegal activities of Tablighi Jamaat. The Tablighi intelligence units are bound to trace addresses of government officials, intelligence workers and its sectarian opponents across Europe. Having reviewed the prevailing threatening situation and illegal activities of Tablighi Jamaat in the Netherlands, General Intelligence and Security Service of the Netherlands (AVID) have also identified a new phase of radicalization in the country. Tablighi Jamaat has also established an extremist and intelligence network in the Netherlands, where its workers have spread in towns and cities. The AVID stressed that Tablighi was a variant of radical Islam and 'manifest themselves in non-violent, radical-Islamic puritan groups'.In its report, South Asia Democratic Forum's paper (Policy Brief 10–Tablighi Jamaat and its role in the Global Jihad. South Asia Democratic Forum 11 December 2020) has reviewed concerns of Portugal intelligence agencies: "Serviço de Informações de Segurança (SIS, Intelligence and Security Service). According to Maria do Céu Pinto, since 2001, the country's intelligence and law enforcing agencies have identified links 'between individuals residing in Portugal and radical Islamic operatives within the ideological network of Al Qaeda, as well as logistical and support activities for terrorism, namely of a criminal nature".[7]

This is an interesting, excruciating and gut-wrenching story of Tablighi Jamaat that preaches and delivers sermons across the globe, but secretly operates as an intelligence agency in India, Pakistan and Bangladesh. The group has been recently banned in some states, while it has changed its intelligence operational mechanism to dance with new tangos in South and Central Asia. The Tablighi Jamaat has been spying for some states since decades, collecting intelligence information from remote areas, terrorist nests, insurgent's centres and neighbouring states. Pakistan's Tablighi Jamaat has established different political and religious intelligence units in state institutions of India, Bangladesh and Pakistan, and appointed its own trained officers, bureaucrats, and political elements to collect money from every corner to facilitate its worldwide intelligence mission. The bureaucracy and leadership of the groups are composed of retired military generals and civil-military intelligence agencies. Experts who have established worldwide contacts with governments, intelligence agencies and extremist organisations are members of Tablighi Jamaat. The group has established its intelligence networks in all mosques of the EU member states, the United States, the Arab world and Africa. The group traces addresses for wanted political workers and critics across EU and South Asia, and brings more young and educated people into its clandestine networks. Former intelligence experts, military generals and militant organizations are the main target of the Tablighi intelligence infrastructure.

Every Pakistani government and every army chief is bound to facilitate this group, participate in its mission, while civilian and military intelligence agencies have been sending their spy agents with its groups to every town, city, and province to collect intelligence information, and trace addresses of political opponents, writers and militant organizations. The Tablighi Jamaat role under the leadership of former ISI Chief General Javed Nasir in Bosnia conflict was crucial by recruiting jihadists to fight the Serbian army. According to Vaibhav Singh's Tweet (04 April 2020), "Lt Gen Javed Nasir, former Chief of ISI is also a Patron of Tablighi Jamaat. Javed Nasir was the man who planned & organised "1993 Mumbai Bomb Blasts". Tablighi Jamaat Members were also responsible for San Bernardino Massacre and Barcelona Bombings Lt Gen Javed Nasir was removed by Nawaz Sharif because he didn't cooperate with CIA in buying back the Stringer Missiles from Afghan Mujahideens. He took it from them & gave it to Terrorists & Pak Army deployed in Kargil Region. He is a close confidant of Parvez Musharraf."[9]

Journalist Qaiser Butt reported to Express Tribune (Islamabad refuses to hand over ex-ISI chief to Bosnia tribunal: The Hague earlier demanded custody of Lt Gen Javed Nasir for his alleged support to Muslim fighters in the 1990s war-September 20, 2011) that Pakistan refused to hand over one of its retired army generals to the International Tribunal of Hague on medical grounds, Qaiser Butt reported. "The tribunal had demanded the custody of a former chief of the Inter-Services Intelligence (ISI), Javed Nasir, a retired lieutenant general, for his alleged support to Muslim fighters of Bosnia against the Serbian army in the 1990s, despite an embargo by the United Nations. Islamabad had informed the court that the former general had 'lost his memory' following a recent road incident, and was, therefore, unable to face any investigation into the matter. Nasir himself was not available for comment. However, his son, Omer Javed, told The Express Tribune that his father was not in service during the Bosnia war in 1993-95, as he had already been "removed from the army". Journalist Qaiser Butt reported.[10] The government of Imran Khan and the Military establishment have been financially supporting Tablighi Jamaat since 2019, while Punjab Assembly once passed a resolution in support of the group. In Britain, France, EU and the United States, the Tablighi Jamaat has appeared on the fringes of several terrorism investigations, leading some to speculate that its political stance simply masked fertile ground for breeding terrorism. The group is the best source of intelligence collection for some states and some western intelligence agencies. Hindustan Times (Pakistan stood in support of Tablighi Jamaat, is Imran Khan going against Saudi Arabia? 24 December 2021) reported Pakistan's resolution in support of Tablighi Jamaat:

"Saudi Arabia's ban on Tablighi Jamaat was fiercely criticised in Pakistan. In the assembly of Punjab province, the most influential province of Pakistan, the legislators have even passed a resolution in support of the Tablighi Jamaat. All the legislators of the party and the opposition, in one voice claimed that Tablighi Jamaat has nothing to do with terrorism. At the same time, Saudi Arabia's Religious Ministry announced the ban, saying that this organization is an entry point of terrorism. Punjab Assembly Speaker Chaudhary Pervez Elahi called a special meeting of the House on Tuesday. During this, MLA Khadija Umar presented a proposal in support of Tablighi Jamaat. The Speaker read out the motion and said that the House agrees with the people promoting trust. He claimed that Tablighi Jamaat has nothing to do with terrorism and their history proves that they have never been involved in such work. Later the motion was passed unanimously by the House. The newspaper reported. Having noted decision of Saudi government, the newspaper noted the Saudi Arabia decision that the group was the entry point of terrorism and it threatened society.[11]

The Saudi Ministry of Islamic Affairs instructed mosques to warn people not to join them in Friday prayers. In a series of tweets, the Ministry said that His Excellency the Minister of Islamic Affairs, Dr. Abdul Latif Al-Alsheikh, urged all mosques to include it in their rituals and to make people aware of the dangers associated with it". As mentioned earlier, some intelligence agencies have been using Tablighi Jamaat for intelligence information collection for years. The Tablighi Jamaat, which means the 'party of Islam's preachers,' organizes gatherings in India, Pakistan and Bangladesh to recruit citizens of these countries and collect money for its secret mission. It was founded in 1926 by the Indian cleric Muhammad Ilyas al-Kandhlawi with an aim to spread Islam to non-Muslims and also to purge the faith from influences of other religions, most notably the Hindu and Christian influences in British India at the time. There are numerous reports in newspapers and journals that highlight different aspects of Tablighi Jamaat in different perspectives. Tablighi Jamaat has established thousands of religious schools in Pakistan, India and Bangladesh to recruit young generations for their missions. They invite educated people from India, Bangladesh, Central Asia and SouthEast Asia and recruit them for their intelligence mission. Analyst and expert, Ashwaq Masoodi (16 September 2013) has noted resentment of governments against the Tablighi Jamaat in Central Asia:

"Tablighi Jamaat finds itself in the news because earlier this year several central Asian countries that were once part of the USSR—Uzbekistan, Tajikistan, Kazakhstan—banned it, largely because they interpret its back to-basics approach to Islam as extremist. A WikiLeaks document released in 2011 suggested that al-Qaeda operatives used the Tablighi Jamaat's headquarters at Nizamuddin in New Delhi as a cover to obtain travel documents and shelter. Some believe the movement is a fertile recruitment ground for extremists. In fact, it has been called the "antechamber of fundamentalism", and "supremacist movement" that promotes isolationism, mostly because the organization doesn't have any constitution or formal registration, which obviously means no one knows who gets in or out of it and no one keeps track of the past or future of the members".[12] Al Jazeera news (Pakistan quarantines 20,000 following Tabligh gathering in Lahore, 6 Apr 2020) in its reports spotlighted more than 20,000 members of Tablighi Jamaat quarantined in Pakistan. Pakistani authorities reported they tested and quarantined those who congregated at the event held by the missionary movement, Tablighi Jamaat, between March 10-12 over fears they might now spread COVID-19 across Pakistan and overseas. Al Jazeera reported more than 100,000 people went to the meeting. More than 7,000 Tablighis were ordered to quarantine in the central Punjab city of Lahore, while in southern Sindh province up to 8,000 Tablighis were quarantined".[13] Networks of terrorist and extremist organizations in Europe are expanding with the arrival of new extremist elements and those who fought in Afghanistan, Iraq and Syria.

There is thousands of ISIS and IS-K recruited elements in France, Germany, Belgium, Netherlands and Italy who participate in holy wars against states and civilization time and again. Tablighi Jamaat is an old master of extremism and intelligence information collection in Asia and Europe that organizes such groups in Europe. Presently its central target is France. The group understands that President Macron government was the enemy of Prophet Muhammad that issued controversial statements in the past. The group represents military establishments of some states and their intelligence infrastructure, and works for the interests of some international intelligence agencies. Business Standard, (02 April 2020), in its recent report about the underwhelming activities of Tablighi Jamaat in Central Asia and Europe has exposed the secret mission of the group: "The organisation's headquarters in Europe, located in Dewsbury, England, was built in 1978- thanks to money from the World Muslim League. And it is not only Italy, in fact, but also France, United Kingdom and USA to have proven links of the organization to Al Qaida and other terror groups. But someway the attention to the group, despite evidences of partnership with a number of jihadi groups, and despite the fact that several famous jihadi have been linked to the organization, is quite loose and the West did not ban the group yet. According to the intelligences of western countries, in fact, Tablighi Jamaat is not a terrorist group in itself but 'only' the "antechamber of terrorism".[14]

They infiltrate mosques and Koranic schools which are gradually reopened to radicalise the local Muslims and transform them into fighters to be sent to war theatres but does not commit any terrorist act itself. Things are different in Russia where Tablighi Jamaat operates differently. Fundamental target of Tablighi Jamaat has been Europe since the 1990s, where the group supports some groups and uses them for intelligence missions. In France, Netherlands, Germany and Spain, the groups use services of some Muslim communities to collect intelligence information. In February 2020, counterterrorism operation in Moscow led to the dismantling of a terrorist cell directly affiliated to Tablighi Jamaat. The Russian Federal Secret Service arrested in fact seven people, both Russian and Central Asians, all actual members of the Tablighi. The cell, according to Russian intelligence, was engaged in various activities, including the search for new followers through a strong campaign of proselytising. Moscow, unlike the Western countries, has banned and outlawed the Tablighi Jamaat activities in the country since 2009, when the organisation was included, on recommendation of the Russian Supreme Court, into the list of terrorist groups monitored by the Kremlin". In 2012, Kazakhstan's law enforcement agencies noticed activities of 205 sarcastic organisations representing Pakistan based Tablighi Jamaat's participation in Kazakhstan's protest raised important questions including its strategic objectives in Central Asian states.

The Tablighi Jamaat facilitates extremist groups in the region and recruits young people for its intelligence mission. In his Eurasia Daily Monitor article, (The Tablighi Jamaat: A Soft Islamization from the Ferghana Valley to Russia's Turkic Regions? The Jamestown Foundation's Eurasia Daily Monitor Volume: 10 Issue: 12, 2013), expert and analyst, Igor Rotar has highlighted activities of Tablighi Jamaat in Central Asia: "Tablighi Jamaat's reach is not limited to Central Asia, however, and its members maintain links with like-minded individuals in the Russian Federation. The main regions of Tablighi Jamaat activity in Russia are Tatarstan and Bashkortostan, which are separated from Kazakhstan by Russia's Orenburg oblast (province). Ethnic Tatars constitute 7.6 percent of the population of the Orenburg oblast; Kazakhs make up six percent, while Bashkirs constitute two percent. The Orenburg oblast is, thus, the inter-link between Turkic ethnic groups living in Russia and Central Asia. At the beginning of Perestroika, some Turkic nationalists told the author that due to this Orenburg link, it would be possible to establish "a Greater Turkestan" from Central Asia to Tatarstan. The Tablighi Jamaat has, indeed, been quite active in the Orenburg oblast since 2010. In September 2012, more than 500 members of the Tablighi Jamaat movement were arrested in Sol-Iletsk district of Orenburg, which borders Kazakhstan. Among those arrested were two leaders of the Tablighi Jamaat's Orenburg branch. During the search of their homes more than 500 copies of religious books with extremist content were confiscated.[15]

An investigation reportedly revealed that Tablighi Jamaat missionaries from the United Arab Emirates, Malaysia and Kazakhstan regularly worked in Kazakhstan (Interfax, September 17, 2012). Notably, ethnic Kazakhs constitute 26 percent of the Sol-Iletsk district's population, while ethnic Tatars make up ten percent (Russian Federation Census, 2010). It is, therefore, possible to conclude that in recent years, the Tablighi Jamaat has successfully established a continuous zone of operations from the Ferghana Valley all the way to the Turkic regions of Russia" (2010 The Jamestown Foundation). In yesteryears, Tablighi Jamaat was profiled as the source of spreading the Covid-19 in India and Pakistan while the group had arranged a large gathering in Nizamuddin area, and in Raiwind Pakistan, in which thousands of its followers participated. Expert and analyst, Sushant Sareen in his recent article (The Tablighi Jamaat tangle, Observer Research Foundation-01 April 2020) has noted outrage of civil society in India over the violation of Covid-19 restrictions by Tablighi Jamaat:

"The outrage being expressed in India over the discovery of a Covid 19 cluster in the capital Delhi's Nizamuddin area where the Tablighi Jamaat followers had gathered from around the world for their annual congregation is entirely justified. According to reports already, 10 deaths and over 300 hospitalisations are being linked to the TJ congregation. Worse, because people had come from all across India, many of the returnees have become carriers of the virus to their states, cities and villages in all four corners of the country. While the blame-game over how the Tablighis brazenly violated government orders against any gathering bigger than 20 people, how foreigners could violate their tourist visas for preaching activity, the irresponsibility and negligence of Jamaat leaders in taking proper action etc. is unavoidable, what matters more is how to contain the damage, if at all this is still possible considering that attendees would have spread out to remote parts of India and perhaps passed on the virus. But the Covid Central Asia is Teetering on the Brink 42 19 havoc wrought by the Tablighi Jamaat is not limited to India alone. The outrage being expressed in India over the discovery of a Covid 19 cluster in the capital Delhi's Nizamuddin area where the Tablighi Jamaat followers had gathered from around the world for their annual congregation is entirely justified".[16]

In Pakistan, the Tablighi Jamaat has been discovered as the biggest intelligence information gathering group. "Despite warnings and entreaties to not hold the annual congregation in Raiwind, on the outskirts of Lahore, the ijtema was held in the second week of March. Similar congregations were held in Khyber Pakhtunkhwa province where videos were circulated scoffing at the dangers posed by the virus, which was called a fraud. Within days, health authorities started discovering Covid 19 patients who could be traced back to the Tablighi congregations". The BBC news report (Tablighi Jamaat: The group blamed for new Covid-19 outbreak in India-02 April 2020) has highlighted the journey and suspicious activities of Tablighi Jamaat in India and Bangladesh. The report also noted Indian government profiling of Tablighi Jamaat as the source of spread of Covid-19: "People who took part in a Tablighi Jamaat function earlier this month walk to board buses taking them to a quarantine facility amid concerns of infection, on day 7 of the 21 day nationwide lockdown imposed by PM Narendra Modi to check the spread of coronavirus, at Nizamuddin West on March 31, 2020 in New Delhi, India. Since then, police have cleared out the hostel where these foreign nationals were staying and quarantined them in another location in Delhi. Efforts are now on in every state to trace and test people who were at the event as the number of Covid-19 cases linked to the event steadily rises. Tablighi Jamaat is now a global religious movement, with followers in more than 80 countries, including Indonesia, Malaysia and the US."[17]

In February 2013, a court in Astana banned Tablighi Jamaat due to its illegal activities. Kazakhstan's Prosecutor-General's Office designated TJ as extremist and all its activities in Kazakhstan. The court cited the ideas that the group has propagated, but it is unclear what specific ideas were found to be extremist. "Faced with the risk of a renewed Islamic insurgency in Central Asia as a result of the conflict in Afghanistan (Crisis Group-2009) and their policy failures, governments are hitting out at radical Islamists, sending more of them to prison for longer. In Kyrgyzstan and Kazakhstan, the main target is Hizb ut-Tahrir (HT), a clandestine political party which aims to create a caliphate in the Muslim world".In the 1990s, different Pakistani extremist groups were fighting in Chechnya to establish Islamic Caliphate there, but Russia crushed their networks. In his article in Telangana Today (A shake-up for Central Asia-14 January 2022), former Ambassador of India to Kazakhstan, Sweden and Latvia, an Executive Council Member at Manohar Parrikar Institute for Defence Studies and Analyses and President, Institute of Global Studies, Ashok Sajjanhar has highlighted networks of extremist groups in Central Asia and noted aspects of events in Kazakhstan in which extremist groups including Tablighi Jamaat participated:

"The involvement and presence of such large numbers of "terrorists, sleeper cells and militants" (almost 20,000 attacked Almaty) is bad news for all countries in the region, particularly India. The forcible seizure of power by the Taliban in Afghanistan in August, 2021, and the departure of US and NATO forces soon thereafter, has imbued a sense of triumphalism in Pakistan and anxiety in the neighbouring countries, particularly Central Asia and India, that terrorist forces will feel emboldened to launch strikes in these countries. It is imperative for all countries in the region to cooperate by sharing real-time intelligence on terrorist activities so that action can be taken against them before they are able to perpetrate such heinous carnage. Kazakhstan is a rich and prosperous country. Notwithstanding its huge ethnic and religious diversity with 135 different nationalities, peace and stability prevail. Since its independence from the Soviet Union in 1991, Kazakhstan has emerged as a role model of cohesion, tranquillity and peaceful development....According to reports, Russia's security establishment, which has been closely monitoring developments in Kazakhstan, appears to have come to the initial conclusion that Pakistan's Tablighi Jamaat in connivance with Afghanistan-trained radicals have carried out these terror attacks in Kazakhstan. Pakistan's Tablighi Jamaat, which has been trying to make inroads in Central Asia, is alleged to have played a role in creating a terror-type atmosphere in Kazakhstan".[18]

It was thought (Indian Narrative, Ashok Sajjanha-12 January 2022) that "if the protesters were demonstrating for reversal of the decision on LPG and for addressing political demands, they would have been mollified by President Tokayev's decision to restore the cap on LPG prices for the next 6 months and by dismissing Prime Minister Askar Mamin on 5th January. However, rather than these actions having any salutary effect on the protesters, the violence, bloodshed and destruction continued to grow rapidly". Attack on US Synagogue authenticated that Pakistan backed terrorism remains a threat to Central Asia. The Journalist, author and a South Asia expert who has written 'Apocalypse Pakistan' Francesca Marino (Quint, 21 Jan 2022) in her analysis noted activities of Pakistani activist Malik Faisal Akram and his affiliation with Tablighi Jamaat:

"Malik Faisal Akram, the 'British citizen' attacker of the Texas synagogue, had travelled 11 times to Jhelum, Pakistan, between 2007 and 2020, to see his relatives and family. Not really. According to investigations, in fact, Malik had joined the Tablighi Jamaat and was travelling with other members of the organisation. News reports, besides the usual comment of "all roads of terrorism lead to Pakistan", highlight once more the very odd position of European governments towards the organisation. In Brescia, Italy, the so called 'cultural centre' run by the Tabligh Eddawa, the missionary branch of Tablighi Jamaat, has been closely monitored for a couple of years now by the Italian intelligence because of the kind of devotees it welcomed and still welcomes. According to the Italian police, in fact, from the 'centre' passed Maulana Tariq Jameel, a member of the Tablighi Jamaat and director of a madrassa in Faisalabad, Pakistan. Zulfikal, arrested in 2015 during a counter-terrorism operation in Sardinia, was, unfortunately, freed because the terms for pre-trial detention expired. He is currently under close monitoring as the Tribunal said there are "valid sources of evidence relating to his supposed financing, direction and liaison with armed groups operating abroad dedicated to the design and implementation of guerrillas and terrorist acts".[19] In yesteryears, Tablighi Jamaat was allowed to inculcate military officers about their mission and recruited missionaries for its international mission. Analyst and expert, Salahuddin Shoaib Choudhury in his article (Pakistani ISI uses Tablighi Jamaat for spreading Islamist jihad, Organizer Newspaper, 28 Dec 2021) noted links between Pakistani intelligence agencies and the Tablighi Jamaat:

"Pakistani spy agency Inter-Service Intelligence (ISI), as well as several jihadist groups such as Al Qaeda, Islamic State and the Taliban, have been using Tablighi Jamaat as the most convenient vessel for spreading religious extremism and Islamist jihad, despite the fact, Pakistan's own security analysts have written in detail about how former missionaries of Tablighi Jamaat have formed some of the most dreaded terror outfits like the Harkat-ul-Mujahideen (HuM). Pakistan's own investigators have said that former members of the Tablighi Jamaat formed the Harkat-ul-Mujahideen. Meanwhile, according to counterterrorism experts, Tablighi Jamaat is being used by notorious Jamaat-e-Islami for spreading religious extremism and anti-India sentiment. There also are indications of deeper. The Kazakhstan Bellyache ties between Tablighis, Palestinian Islamic Jihad and Hamad. Recently, Saudi Arabia has banned the activities of Tablighi Jamaat and alerted every mosque and religious centres in the country to report any activities of Tablighis. The Saudi authorities termed Tablighi Jamaat a gate to terrorism while prohibiting all its activities on Saudi soil. In several countries around the world, Tablighi Jamaat is considered the antechamber of terrorism and spreads religious hatred. While several Muslim nations, including Saudi Arabia, are banning the activities of Tablighi Jamaat".[20]

Moreover, the EU today news report (Europe & US terror fears over Tablighi Jamaat Islamic group, 26 August 2020) also noted clandestine activities of Tablighi Jamaat in Europe and the United States. As of 2007, it was estimated that 10,000 Tablighi Jamaat members could be found in Kyrgyzstan, a presence largely driven by Pakistani migrants. The Group's activities in Kyrgyzstan are of particular interest: "The group is banned in a number of post-Soviet states, notably Russia, and Central Asian countries such as Uzbekistan, Tajikistan and Kazakhstan, where its puritanical preaching is viewed as extremist. As of 2007, it was estimated that 10,000 Tablighi Jamaat members could be found in Kyrgyzstan, a presence largely driven by Pakistani migrants. The Group's activities in Kyrgyzstan are of particular interest. There is an opinion that Tablighi Jamaat is used by the authorities to distract society from acute socio-economic problems. In the country Tablighi Jamaat plays a special role during the electoral period because the leadership of the Spiritual Board of Muslims of Kyrgyzstan largely adheres to the ideas of Tablighi Jamaat. Some of the terrorists involved in the 9/11 terrorist attack had reportedly stayed in the premises of the Tablighi Jamaat center in New Delhi. Terrorist Syed Rizwan Farook, involved in the 2015 San Bernardino, California attack which left 16 innocent people dead and 22 injured, was a student of the teachings of Tablighi Jamaat".[21]

On 05 January 2022, the Kazakhstan government banned the internet in order to meet the challenges of domestic turmoil and foreign-sponsored violence. There were news reports that Tablighi Jamaat of Pakistan, the IS Khorasan and Lashkar-e-Taiba were involved in violence in Kazakhstan. The abrupt withdrawal of US forces from Afghanistan left behind the strongest networks of Islamic State of Khorasan, Lashkar-e-Taiba and Taliban". According to former Interior Minister of Pakistan, Dr. Rahman Malik; "more than 80,000 young religious fighters from Southern Punjab province of Pakistan have already joined the IS-Khorasan terrorist group". Analyst and expert, Catherine Putz in her article (Curious Case of the Kyrgyz Jazzman Detained in Kazakhstan: The bizarre story illustrates a wider set of concerns as the Kazakh government claims to have arrested nearly 8,000 people in the wake of a week of chaos in Kazakhstan-The Central Asia is Teetering on the Brink. Diplomat, 11 January 2022) has highlighted some aspects of Kazakhstan violence:

"The bizarre story illustrates a wider set of concerns as the Kazakh government claims to have arrested nearly 8,000 people in the wake of a week of chaos in Kazakhstan. The internet in Kazakhstan remains heavily restricted, with access seemingly limited to the morning hour's local time in Almaty and larger windows of time elsewhere. This has the effect of limiting the sharing of information by any sources other than the government, which is now pushing a remarkable narrative peopled by "sleeper cells" of foreign-trained terrorists. In a speech on January 10 to an emergency session of the Collective Security Treaty Organization (CSTO), which had deployed troops for the first time ever as an organisation to Kazakhstan, Kazakh President Kassym-Jomart Tokayev doubled down on a familiar narrative: That the violence seen in Almaty was the result of "Religious radicals, criminals, outright thugs, looters and petty hooligans" who "filled the streets as if on cue" after the demands of peaceful protesters had been met by the government. "I can tell you in all certainty that terrorists, including foreign fighters, were directly involved in the aggression against Kazakhstan," he also said, pushing the plot off a steep cliff in continuing: "It was not a coincidence that the criminals attacked morgues at night to collect and drive away with the corpses of their dead accomplices. They also took the corpses of fighters from the battlefield."[22]

Moreover, expert and analyst, Dr. Afsana Mammadova noted (Kazakhstan on the threshold: geostrategic competition or geopolitical reality, Modern diplomacy. January 12, 2022) political and religious aspects of violence in Kazakhstan and highlighted the role of Collective security in controlling violence: "In the January clashes, the role of several actors is not excluded. The spread of peaceful demonstrations in the Mangistau region to the larger cities of Kazakhstan, with the help of some trained gangs, led to riots, looting and murders. The protest moved away from the initial demands for lower fuel prices. It continued with appeals for the resignation of the President and government, implementation of political reforms, the recognition of the criminalization of the USSR administration, etc. The violation of the "red line of security" of the government of Kazakhstan gave impetus to the deployment of the CSTO peacekeeping forces. Although there was no external threat to the integrity of Kazakhstan, the introduction of the Allied troops exceeded the expectations of not only the West but also the countries of the region. The removal of Nursultan Nazarbayev from the post of life-long head of the Security Council, the demonstrative The Kazakhstan Bellyache demolition of his bust, the dismissal of his adherents and the initiation of a criminal case against his associates – all this "purge" carried out by Tokayev is undoubtedly a well-thought-out staging aimed at ending Nazarbayev's political era and the beginning of a new era in the person of Russophile Tokayev."[23]

On 50 January, 2022, Kazak authorities told newspapers and electronic media that over 400 businesses were damaged by terrorist groups, while more than 200 people had been arrested. The Economic Times in its report noted that Tablighi Jamaat and Taliban sent their fighters to Kazakhstan. The newspaper reported that Hezb Tehrer and Tablighi Jamaat were in contact with Kazak extremist groups during violent protest. Luca Anceschi, professor of Eurasian Studies at the University of Glasgow in his recent report (Carnegie Europe, 11 January 2022) noted inequality and democratic deficit: "After the process of leadership change staged by the regime in 2019, Kazakhstan's democratic deficit remained significant. Its stagnating economy led to massive inequality across social classes, regions, and age groups. Kazakhstani society at large became exasperated by the regime's ultimate failure to deliver on its political and economic promises".[24]

Chapter 4

Imran Khan, Military Establishment and the Inter-Services Intelligence

Pakistani Prime Minister Imran Khan was removed from his office by ISI and the army. The ISI and the army in the past had threatened former Prime Minister Mian Nawaz Sharif and President Zardari of dire consequences when they decided to bring ISI under democratic control. The same happened with Imran Khan when he decided to remove the Army Chief General Bajwa. Non-resident scholar in the South Asia Program at the Carnegie Endowment for International Peace, James Schwemlein in his paper noted: "Some of Pakistan's closest historical partners—China, Saudi Arabia, the United Arab Emirates, and Turkey among them—were uncomfortable with Khan's freewheeling, personal style of diplomacy. While each of these relationships is led by the Pakistan Army, the return of a more well-known and experienced interlocutor on the civilian side is likely to be a boon, which will be particularly important as the government returns to the IMF, seeks to renegotiate the terms of foreign loans to reduce the growing pressure of debt service payments, and continues to negotiate to purchase oil and natural gas. Shehbaz Sharif has committed to visiting Saudi Arabia and China soon, in a nod toward their importance as strategic partners. The other major relationship to mention is with India. In recent years, the Indian government and the Pakistan Army have made important, quiet overtures aimed at improving ties. Sharif will be supportive of this effort, but particularly ahead of the general election, there is likely to be little appetite to make accommodations that could progress talks with India".[1]

With almost no hope left for an embattled Imran Khan to save his government from collapsing, Pakistan's Army Chief General Bajwa and Inter-Services Intelligence (ISI) head Lieutenant-General Nadeem Anjum reached the Prime Minister's official residence in Islamabad for a special meeting. Imran Khan was adamant about telling the Pakistan army for a

U-Turn, but the army refused. Press Trust of India (24 June 2022) reported Imran Khan's address to a seminar in Islamabad. He clarified that he never planned on appointing an army chief of his own choice in November 2022, when the tenure of General Bajwa is expired.[2] However, on 06 July 2022, Press Trust of India noted that the chief of Pakistan's spy agency-ISI had issued strict orders to all commanders to stay away from politics following directives from Army Chief Gen Qamar Javed Bajwa to offset a smear campaign against the military by ousted Prime Minister Imran Khan's party. Lieutenant General Nadeem Anjum, Director General (DG) of Pakistan's Inter-Services Intelligence (ISI), personally issued the instructions to his subordinates; Express Tribune newspaper reported. On 03 July 2022, Press Trust of India reported the humiliation of a senior Pakistani journalist and political analyst by unidentified masked men, who also tore his clothes, as he left his office. Ayaz Amir, 73, was returning home after recording his television show for Dunya News TV channel, where he works as a senior analyst, when unknown persons stopped his car. The attackers then manhandled him and also tortured his driver before fleeing from the scene.[3]

Jihadist general and former chief of ISI, Faiz Hamid declared support for Imran Khan, and revealed rifts in Pak military. The split in an apparently cohesive Pakistani army is getting wider by the day as Lt. General (retired) Zaheerul Islam, the former chief of Pakistan's spy agency, the Inter-Services Intelligence (ISI) came out openly in support of the ousted Prime Minister Imran Khan. There are strong "rumours" that Imran Khan selected the ex- ISI boss as a PTI candidate for the next general elections. The PTI leaders have denied the speculation, but Islam was seen campaigning for a PTI candidate in a by-election in Rawalpindi for the Pakistani National Assembly. Analyst and commentator, Dibakar Dutta, (10 April 2022) in his articles, noted the humiliation and torture of Imran Khan by General Bajwa:

"On Sunday (April 10) morning, social media was rife with claims that Pakistani Chief of Army Staff (COAS) General Qamar Bajwa roughed up Prime Minister Imran Khan at his residence on Saturday night for allegedly trying to remove him and changing the leadership of the Pakistani army. The development comes at a time when Pakistan is going through a period of political turmoil, with the Imran Khan government failing to win the no-confidence motion. New PM Shehbaz Sharif is likely to take office soon and form a new government. One Twitter user Ali claimed, "Around 10:00 at night PM de-notified Gen Bajwa. Meanwhile, a helicopter arrived at PM House. At PM House, soldiers stopped the speaker in the waiting room. Imran was waiting for Gen Faiz but Gen Bajwa himself was in the helicopter. (The) meeting started in the room and it was a very bad one." Another Pakistani Twitter user alleged, "He didn't hand over. He was forced out at gunpoint. Bajwa and DGISI came in helicopter, entered PM House and misbehaved with PM. It is a coup with the civilian façade. America, 3 stooges, judges, and the Army chief were complicit. III Brigade was deployed". Saleem Akhtar in his Tweet noted that General Bajwa and the ISI Chief came in a helicopter, entered the PM house and misbehaved with PM.....A Twitter user Zameer Afaqi claimed."[4]

On 17 July 2022, Dawn newspaper reported Imran Khan's regret on the imbalance in civil-military relations, as he blamed previous PPP and PML-N governments for ceding space to the army to 'save their skin' in corruption cases. The former Prime Minister made these remarks at a seminar on freedom of expression, a day ahead of crucial by-polls in Punjab, where his party was contesting on 20 Punjab Assembly seats across the province. "Because of this imbalance, a situation has developed that [now] the establishment isn't realising [the consequences of] the actions it is committing," he said, while referring to a crackdown against his party following his ouster as a result of the no-confidence motion. "We cannot afford a weak army... we have to protect it. If the distance between the army and the public keeps increasing, which it is, then it will eventually harm the army and Pakistan. "Dawn reported. The newspaper also reported Imran Khan's remarks about the enforced disappearances and a clampdown on journalists under his regime and said that his government had nothing to do with whisking people away or restrictions on media. "I was never afraid of media… [I] was the most criticised PM… [yet] I never tried to bribe journalists or take action against them," the ex-PM added. Dawn reported.[5]

In a recent television interview, the speaker of the Provincial Assembly of Punjab, Chuodhry Pervez Elahi, one of Khan's own allies, openly blamed the military for the government's collapse. He said in an interview in Urdu on HUM television Pakistan, "... they (the military) kept changing Khan's nappies all the time instead of providing him opportunities to learn politics and the art of governance". He noted. However, he also noted the failure of the hybrid Khan-military regime miserably, worsening instability in the country and leaving a legacy of high inflation, especially food inflation, dwindling foreign reserves and increasing deficits. In addition to the economic crisis, Pakistan faces ongoing challenges, including balancing global pressure to persuade the Taliban in neighbouring Afghanistan to meet human rights commitments while trying to limit instability and terrorism within the country. Previously, the onus for the failure of Pakistan's hybrid regimes has fallen on civilian governments". Dr Nadeem Malik Noted.

The Army has failed to develop a true ethnic representation process or to motivate Baloch and Sindhis to join the ranks of the armed forces. Every major attack on a military installation in the country bears clear marks of collusion by elements from within. Many Pakistan Air Force (PAF) and army personnel, including six officers, were convicted for attempts on the life of General Pervez Musharraf in December 2003, when he was the country's President. Recent events in Kazakhstan and Tajikistan have raised the prospect of Pakistan based extremist and jihadist groups using biological, radiological and chemical weapons against military installations and critical national infrastructure in both states. Russia and Indian are vulnerable to such attacks by these terrorist groups who received military training in the US Army bases in Afghanistan and Pakistan. The greatest threat to the national security of India stems from the business of nuclear smuggling. Increasingly sophisticated chemical and biological weapons are accessible to these organizations and ISIS and their allies, which is a matter of great concern.

These groups can use more sophisticated conventional weapons as well as chemical and biological agents in the near future in India and Russia. In July 2018, five Tajik men killed four foreign cyclists in a car-ramming attack, accompanied by an on-foot gun and knife assault in the Khatlon province of Tajikistan. The presence of Daesh in Iraq and Tablighi Jamaat in India and participation of these groups in Kashmir has prompted consternation in India. These terrorists have Salafi-Wahhabi inclinations and are among the backers of al-Qaeda, al-Nusra Front, and Daesh group. The ISIS and Pakistan based terrorist groups seek biological and nuclear weapons to use it against India in Kashmir. The modus operandi of ISIS inspired individuals are diverse and show no moral restraints–as recent attacks in Kashmir demonstrated. The use of biological and chemical weapons by terrorists has prompted huge fatalities in Iraq and Syria. However, preventing dangerous materials from falling into the hands Pakistani terrorist groups, and Central Asia extremists is a complex challenge to the national security of India and Afghanistan.

The weak and fragile government of Imran Khan was unable to introduce intelligence reform as the ISI doesn't allow civilian intelligence to operate independently. The ISI is the dominant actor in Pakistan's political life, despite some improvements in civil-military relations in recent years. The ISI supports sectarian groups in Pakistan who had emerged from the conflict in Afghanistan and by the US invasion in the country. The ISI first dematerialized the IB and FIA, then controlled the whole process of terrorist's infiltration into India and Afghanistan, and received billions dollars from NATO and the United States. The ISI proxies carried out suicide attack in Afghanistan and India. On 13 February 2015, General Musharraf admitted that he had instructed the ISI to recruit suicide bomber and organize attacks against Afghan army and government institutions to force the Karzai administration to close unnecessary diplomatic presence of India in Afghanistan. When the ISI atrocities intensified in Afghanistan after the announcement of Biden administration, and its policy of confrontation failed, Pakistan relinquished supporting Kashmir and allowed India to properly control and oversee it. The army also commenced peace efforts in Afghanistan on the one hand and attacked different districts and provinces of the country to save its strategic depth on the other. Blabbermouth, tattler, double-crosser and whistle-blowers within civilian intelligence kicked up one's heel and raised their voices against the total control of ISI and the IB managements.

Analyst and expert, F.M. Shakil in his article (The growing 'tug-of-war' between Pakistan's spy agencies: Conflict between the civilian Intelligence Bureau (IB), and the military's Inter-Services Intelligence (ISI) is at boiling point, with the former accused of overstepping constitutional bounds, Asia Times. 04 October 2017) has highlighted the tug-of-war between the ISI and the Intelligence Bureau (IB): "The bubbling rivalry between the IB and ISI boiled over in June this year when a Joint Investigation Team (JIT) probing alleged money laundering by the Sharif family made a written complaint to the Supreme Court that the IB was wiretapping JIT members, including ISI and Military Intelligence (MI) personnel. Other JIT members from the National Accountability Bureau (NAB), the Federal Investigation Agency (FIA), the State Bank of Pakistan (SBP) and the Security & Exchange Commission of Pakistan (SECP) were also alleged to have had their phones bugged. The JIT further reported that the IB was hampering its inquiries, adding that military-led intelligence agencies were not on "good terms" with the IB. It said the IB had collected intelligence on members of the JIT from the National Database and Registration Authority (NADRA) and presented it to Nawaz to use against them. The Supreme Court inquired how the IB came to be working for a "private person" instead of the state, adding that – as it owed its loyalty to the latter – it seemed, prima facie, to have been misused"[6]

The ISI and military intelligence death squads are making things worse as they target civilian populations particularly Pashtun and Baloch activists with impunity. These squads have killed prominent Pashtun and Baloch leaders but no independent investigation was allowed to find out the real story behind these killings. The former terrorist leader and member of TTP spokesman Ehsanullah Ehsan revealed that the Pakistan army asked him to lead a squad. On 13 August 2020, he revealed that Pakistani authorities had given him a hit list of people who they would like to be killed in Khyber Pakhtunkhwa.In an audio, he claimed that after some time of his surrender he was given the list of prominent voices in order to facilitate Pakistan in eliminating rogue elements. Daily Times reported his confession audio, in which he admitted: "I was asked to lead a death squad and accept killing of the listed people from Khyber Pakhtunkhwa and Pashtuns from all walks of life including journalists. In the audio, he talked about his conversations with ISI and the parleys that took place. Ehsanullah Ehsan (Liaqat Ali) was a former spokesman of Tehreek-e-Taliban Pakistan (TTP) and Jamaat-ul-Ahrar. In April 2017, Inter-Services Public Relations (ISPR) Director-General Asif Ghafoor announced that Ehsan had surrendered himself to Pakistan's security agencies. In early February 2020, Ehsanullah claimed that escaped from the custody of Pakistani Agencies.[7]

The Sunday Guardian (06 September, 2020) reported Mr. Ehsanullah Ehsan conversation with Taliban leader Mullah Wali-ur-Rahman: "Maulana Wali-ur-Rehman took a letter out of the envelope and gave it to me and told me to read it. I opened the letter and read it aloud. After doing so, Maulana Wali-ur-Rehman said to me, "You must have known why you were called in an emergency for this meeting." I smiled and said, "Yes, I know." The letter I read was written by the DG ISI, General Shuja Pasha to Maulana Wali-ur-Rehman Mehsud. In it, General Shuja Pasha made an offer to the TTP leadership that if the TTP gave up its armed struggle against Pakistan, the ISI would not only provide them with a safe passage against NATO forces in Afghanistan but also provide financial and military support in every possible way. In this letter, General Shuja Pasha also praised the strength and capabilities of the TTP and called the TTP a necessity for Pakistan. He wrote that we should work together to remove the misunderstandings between the Pakistan army and the TTP and work together to drive the great enemy US (America) and NATO out of Afghanistan.[8]

General Pasha had also proposed if TTP accepted the demands, the TTP would not just be able to demonstrate its abilities in Waziristan but the whole of Pakistan would be open for the TTP and that the cadre of

TTP and their children would be able to work in this country by getting education from educational institutions in Islamabad and Peshawar...... In this detailed letter, General Shuja Pasha had repeatedly referred to the Indian "occupation" of and "atrocities" in Kashmir. He had written to Maulana Wali-ur-Rehman Sahib, saying that his forefathers had fought many wars for the independence of Kashmir and had made many sacrifices because they were true and patriotic Pakistanis. He, in the letter, had added that he should also join the Pakistan army in the "Ghazwa e Hind" war against India, because the war against India is a true and just jihad against the real infidels and polytheists. He also mentioned some Pakistan-backed organizations (Lashker-e-Tayyaba and Jaish-e-Mohammad) that were fighting against India in Kashmir and said that despite all the international pressure, Pakistan army was helping them because they were fighting for Pakistan.[9]

In books and newspapers, there are stories about the failure of intelligence agencies in Pakistan to undermine terrorism and extremism. Recruitment from the business community, wealthy and landlord societies, generals and politicians for intelligence agencies prompted bureaucratic culture. Intelligentsias and political circles have often pointed to the fact that involvement of the agency in political confrontations badly affected its professional credibility. Some circles are trying to radicalize agencies, but the big concern is that all military, civilian and policing agencies have already 'purified' their souls in Tablighi congregations in Raiwind. Sectarian elements within the IB and ISI ranks are purveying secret information about the planning of political parties and military leadership, to their favourite religious and political leaders. Secondly, military intelligence agencies do not cooperate with civilian intelligence agencies on national security issues.

The challenges of democratic consolidation and security sector reform lies in the fact that in Pakistan, there is little public awareness about the function and operation of intelligence agencies. Major political and religious parties have no basic knowledge of the organization of intelligence. For this reason, this book will be the prime source of knowledge for politicians and civil society-containing basic knowledge of the manner of intelligence operation and its role in politics. Thus, ignorance about intelligence communities is combined with fear, which perpetuates inadequate dissemination of information. In modern states, security and intelligence agencies play a vital role in support of the government in its domestic, defence and foreign policies by supplying and analyzing relevant intelligence and countering specified threats. Over the last two decades, the role and scale of Pakistan's intelligence agencies has grown over and above their prescribed functions, to the degree that their operations, often undercover and at odds even with each other, have earned them the reputation of being a "State within a State". In most parts of the country, intelligence information collection faced numerous difficulties since the Taliban and other militant groups returned to important strategic locations. Having faced serious difficulties in dealing with insurgent forces in Balochistan and Waziristan, the agencies started translating their anger into the killing and kidnapping of innocent civilians with impunity. A secret war goes on between the ISI, and the IB which paints a murky picture of concordance and cooperation. It is known that the officials from the military's ISI agency had their phone calls eavesdropped at the height of civil-military tension in 2014.

Chapter 5

The ISI Political Role and its War against Civilian Intelligence

Communication and interconnection, and knit-togetherness between military and civilian intelligence agencies in Pakistan have never been companionable since 1977 when General Zia dethroned Prime Minister Zulfiqar Ali Bhutto in a coup d'état. Military government immediately set a motion to reorganize the weak, poor and unprofessional military intelligence agencies (the ISI and MI), while dematerializing civilian agencies (IB, Special Branch and FIA). The IB and FIA became part of the ISI war against PPP politicians. They were now the ears and eyes of the military government. In 1979, after the Soviet invasion of Afghanistan, the ISI and MI were restrained and encumbered the fun and game to train Afghans and transport them to Afghanistan for fight against the Soviet forces. As per my personal attainment, more than 80 percent of ISI officers and field informers had no access to social media and newspapers in the 1980s. They were honest and stalwart but their communication with headquarters was only by post and main landline-telephone. Because mobile communication was absent from the country, they could not visit the houses of Ministers, landlords, business lords, industrialists and parliamentarians for investigation purposes because of their lack of education and culture of inferiority complex. They were non-technical, unschooled, untutored, uninformed and unacquainted to enter into pontification with journalists and politicians.[1]

In the 1980s and 1990s, the ISI and MI retrieved professional training from the CIA and Pentagon and obtained the best experience of intelligence information collection in war and peace. The intelligence bureau (IB) became weak and dematerialized when its management received 70 percent of posting from military establishment to further skeletal the civilian intelligence infrastructure, and use it against civilian society, politicians, and dissidents. The IB was far weak and incapacitated on account of inattention of military establishment, lack of funds, and intelligence information collection equipment. The IB had become fully militarized and its civilian operational mechanism was copied from military intelligence. Thus, the culture of civilian intelligence demonstration was undermined. The ISI and IB were packed with Mujahideen and Taliban, and their commanders were receiving instructions from sectarian organizations and Tablighi Jamaat.[2]

Pakistan's Intelligence Bureau was established by Major General Sir Charles MacGregor in 1885 in order to make military forces professional and competent by purveying them with fresh intelligence information. After the partition, the IB played a crucial role in protecting the state and security, and tried to strengthen its civilian culture of intelligence information collection. It also played a professional role in 1965 and 1971 wars by keeping the army, government and politicians updated about the activities of Indian forces. The IB was initially Pakistan's main and bigger intelligence agency with the responsibility for strategic and foreign intelligence. Between 1950 and 1980, the IB was monitoring politicians, dissidents, terrorists and emerging developments in Bangladesh and India. The agency also secretly informed Prime Minister Zulfiqar Ali Bhutto of the coup organized by General Gul Hassan Khan, Marshal Abdul Rahim, and preparations of General Zia-ul-Haq to dethrone Prime Minister Bhutto. The Zia military government deeply concentrated on strengthening the ISI to monitor politicians, but enfeebled the Intelligence Bureau (IB) and divided its infrastructure between military and civilian units. In the 1990s, democratic governments helped the IB in gaining international reputation. In 1996, the IB started monitoring and controlling information dissemination via mail, wire, or electronic medium.[3]

The European Asylum Support Office (16 October 2018) in its report noted that 'civilian candidates for the posts of Directorate General of ISI had to pass through a transparent and systematic process comprising written tests, interviews, medical examinations and, in some cases, intelligence and psychological tests as well. Security clearance of the selected candidates is carried out by the vetting agency of the ISI, keeping in view the standards and peculiar requirements in accordance with the mandate of the Directorate. A panel of highly qualified senior officers select the candidates keeping in view the sensitive nature of jobs to be assigned/performed, and the candidates are tested/interviewed with particular emphasis on their potential, trends, zeal, devotion, dedication and psychological suitability required for the job. It is, therefore, in the larger interest of the country to make the recruitment of the posts of Directorate General ISI by the department itself instead of FPSC.[4]

The IB experienced underwhelming ball-games under the shade of military establishment. After the butt-end of military government and Soviet occupation of Afghanistan, civilian intelligence infrastructure was near to disintegration and sinking fast. Its well-trained senior officers had superannuated. When Benazir Bhutto assumed responsibilities as a civilian Prime Minister, she was still unable to reinvent the IB against the willpower of the ISI and military establishment. She was helpless and with hands tied. Mian Nawaz Sharif was upraised by the military establishment as a future Prime Minister. She was designated as an anti-state and India's-RAW agent. Mian Nawaz Sharif assumed power with the help of ISI, General Hamid Gul and Osama Bin Laden in 1997, and served until his removal in 1999 by military takeover and was tried in a plane hijacking case. The ISI and military establishment were not happy with Nawaz Sharif and his ISI chief General Javed Nasir (member of Tablighi Jamaat of Pakistan). General Javed Nasir supplied weapons to Muslim fighters in Bosnia. Miltablishment and Musharraf decided to sideline Nawaz Sharif through a military coup in 1999 after they failed to defeat the Indian army in Kargil. Thus, Nawaz Sharif was dethroned and forced to take refuge in Saudi Arabia.[5]

However, Asif Ali Zardari served as the 11th President of Pakistan from 2008 to 2013, and remained a strong US ally in the war on terrorism in Afghanistan, notwithstanding public disapproval in the United States following the Raymond Davis affairs and the NATO attack in Salala check post in 2011. President Zardari never supported ISI's involvement in politics. He directed the Interior Ministry to bring ISI under democratic control, but faced a disheartening situation. The ISI threatened him with dire consequences. On 07 June 2013, Sharif was sworn in again for an unprecedented third term, but faced numerous challenges, including military establishment, the ISI and US drone strikes against civilian population in Pakistan's tribal regions. After he assumed power, Tehrik Insaf and Thahir Qadri arranged a protest movement with the support of ISI, while civilian intelligence was supporting Nawaz Sharif. The ISI and military establishment arranged a sit-in of 2500 radicalized elements in 2016. On 28 July 2017, Prime Minister Nawaz Sharif was disqualified in a fake Aqama case by the court. Thus, Imran Khan Niazi became the Prime Minister of Pakistan in 2018. Mr. Imran Khan was crippled when foreign and security policy was controlled by the military establishment, and appointed more than 400 military experts on various civilian posts. He was also supported by the ISI and GHQ, but he never gave importance to the IB and demonstrated single-mindedness in the dematerialization of civilian agency.[6]

The weak and fragile government of Imran Khan has been unable to introduce intelligence reform as the ISI doesn't allow civilian intelligence to operate independently. The ISI is the dominant actor in Pakistan's political life, despite some improvements in civil-military relations in recent years. The agency officers use secret funds for their personal and family expenditures. The ISI supports sectarian groups in Pakistan who had emerged from the conflict in Afghanistan and by the US invasion in the country. The ISI first dematerialized the IB and FIA, then controlled the whole process of terrorist's infiltration into India and Afghanistan, and received billions dollars from NATO and the United States, but never shared the cake with both IB and FIA, and their experts were implicated in different cases. The ISI proxies carried out suicide attack in Afghanistan and India. On 13 February 2015, General Musharraf admitted that he had instructed the ISI to recruit suicide bomber and organize attacks against Afghan army and government institutions to force the Karzai administration to close unnecessary diplomatic presence of India in Afghanistan. When the ISI atrocities intensified in Afghanistan after the announcement of the Biden administration, and its policy of confrontation failed, Pakistan relinquished supporting Kashmir and allowed India to properly control and oversee it. The army also commenced peace efforts in Afghanistan. Blabbermouth, tattler, double-crosser and whistleblowers within civilian intelligence kicked up one's heel and raised their voices against the total control of ISI and its war crimes in Afghanistan.[7]

The complex reciprocation among the internal and external forces fashioning Pakistan today call on to an in-depth evaluation of their influence on the country's future- in the context of both continued state stability and Pakistan's potential to jump-start broader security priorities in the region. Established in 1948, the ISI was tasked with acquiring intelligence of strategic interests and assessing the intensity of foreign threats, but political and military stakeholders used the agency adversely, and painted a consternating picture of its working environment. The civilian intelligence agency-Intelligence Bureau (IB) has been gradually neglected, humiliated and enfeebled due to the consecutive military rule and weak democratic governments. Serving and retired military officers were being appointed in increasing numbers to senior posts in the IB, including to the post of

DG. In the 1990s, the IB remained actively involved to curb sectarianism and fundamentalism in the country. Many of its operations were directed towards infiltration, conducting espionage, counterespionage, and providing key information on terrorist organizations.[8]

War of strength between the ISI and Intelligence Bureau (IB) has been reported time and again by Pakistani newspapers to manifest that a decade-long fight of state intelligence agencies might jeopardize the national security of the state that hitherto affianced with neighbours in geographical altercations. The IB headquarters in Punjab has customarily been looted and plundered by the ISI commando groups in 1980s, 1990s and 2000s, and all secret records of domestic and international intelligence information was despoiled. The rough and tumble of intelligence information technology between the two secret agencies brought shame to the country when ISI refused to share that technology with the IB management. Once, a former DG of Intelligence Bureau chronicled the real story of controversial intelligence technology in an hour long meeting with me in his Lahore headquarter. By reading that draft, I realized the sensitivity of the war of power between the ISI, IM, IB and FIA. However, a former Joint Director (My close friend) evinced a critical document about the ISI's political demonstrations and its illegal interference in civilian institutions and government. He told me that ISI and military establishment bribe judges and media owners in cases of their own interests.[9]

The ISI in 2017, recruited a serving Assistant Sub-Inspector (ASI) of IB, Malik Mukhtar Ahmed Shahzad, who filed a petition before the Islamabad High Court (IHC) requesting it to refer the matter to the Inter-Services Intelligence (ISI) for a thorough probe. The purpose of that petition was to further dematerialize the IB. Mr. Shahzad said he purveyed intelligence report to the management against terrorist groups of Uzbekistan, Iran, Afghanistan, Syria and India. Malik noted that upon a thorough intelligence gathering process, it transpired that certain high officials of the IB themselves were directly involved with the terrorist organizations having linkages with hostile enemy intelligence agencies. However, the IB circulated a list of 37 Lawmakers who had established secret interconnection with ISI to update the agency about the intentions of Prime Minister Nawaz Sharif and his close colleagues. Mian Nawaz Sharif later on directed Law Minister Hamid to take action against the channel through the Pakistan Electronic Media Regulatory Authority. Moreover, DG IB Aftab Sultan openly declared war against the illegal interference of ISI in government's decision making process, and visited Nawaz Sharif in London.[10]

Dawn newspaper reported Islamabad High Court Registrar's Office fixation of the petition before Justice Aamer Farooq who referred the case to IHC Chief Justice Mohammad Anwar Khan Kasi, with a note that the matter should be transferred to Justice Shaukat Aziz Siddiqui since an identical matter was pending in his court. In the petition filed through his counsel Masroor Shah, Mr. Shahzad said he joined the IB in 2007, and that he "reported against various terrorist groups having roots in Uzbekistan, Iran, Afghanistan, Syria and India". The ASI told the court he reported against terrorist groups from various countries, but no action was taken: "However, to the petitioner's utter dismay, no action has never been taken by IB in this respect despite concrete evidence provided to it in the form of the intelligence reports", the petition says. "Upon thorough intelligence gathering process, it transpired that certain high officials of the IB themselves are directly involved with the terrorist organizations having linkages with hostile enemy intelligence agencies", the petition reads. It goes on to say that the matter was even reported to the IB director general, who also did not take any steps. It says some IB officials travelled to Israel and had direct links with Afghan intelligence which, it was later found, had links with another terrorist group from Kazakhstan. "These terrorists used to disguise themselves as citrus dealers in Kot-Momin and Bhalwal, Sargodha. The business was a mere camouflage," the petition said.[11]

Moreover, the petition revealed that the son of Joint Director IB (Punjab) had established links with these terror groups. The petition uncovered that some officials of Afghan and Iranian intelligence used to take refuge in the places of the citrus dealers. The petition named certain IB's officials who were on the payroll of foreign intelligence agencies which included a Joint Director General, Directors and Deputy Directors. The petitioner said: "Senior IB officials also facilitate Afghan nationals in getting Pakistani nationality. Mr. Shahzad said he "has been running from pillar to post including approaching the Prime Minister of Pakistan to raise this issue of national security and protection of lives of the citizens of this country but in vain." The petitioner requested the court that the issue of connivance, complacency and involvement of officials of IB and other senior bureaucrats raised in the petition may graciously be entrusted to ISI for investigation. Dawn reported that the Intelligence Bureau (IB) also came under attack by a Joint Investigation Team (JIT) consisting of officials from ISI, Military Intelligence and officials from other departments for 'hampering the investigation' into the assets of former Prime Minister Nawaz Sharif's family. The Intelligence Bureau (IB) was accused by one of its own spies of "protecting" terrorists. That petition prompted misunderstandings between the ISI and the Intelligence Bureau (IB).[12]

The unending resultant tussle between civilian and military intelligence agencies forced former Prime Minister Nawaz Sharif to restructure the IB and make it more effective to counter ISI's influence in political institutions. The Prime Minister allocated huge funds to the IB to recruit and employ more agents to meet the country's internal and external challenges. The greatest challenge Nawaz Sharif faced was on the national security front, where he failed to take control of the security policy of Kashmir and Afghanistan. The miltablishment was not happy with his democratic intentions. The Intelligence Bureau is the country's main civilian intelligence agency that functions under the direct control of the Prime Minister, tackling terrorism, insurgency and extremism. Over the last four decades, the ISI operated in changing security environment, but the agency mostly targeted democracy and political parties, strengthened miltablishment and its illegal business. The intelligence community of Pakistan was once described by the daily Frontier Post (May 18, 1994) as an invisible government, and by the Daily Dawn (April 25, 1994)[16] as secret godfathers consisting of the Intelligence Bureau (IB) and the ISI. While the IB comes under the Interior Minister, the ISI is part of the Ministry of Defence (MOD). Each wing of the Armed Forces maintains its own intelligence directorate. After the PTI Chief Imran Khan became Prime Minister, the IB started dancing to his tango. Analyst Azaz Syed (28 September 2018) noted some developments within the intelligence infrastructure as Prime Minister Imran Khan restructured the agency and fitted it to the recurrent nature of his Charleston:

"Amid a major reshuffle within the premier civilian intelligence outfit, the Intelligence Bureau (IB) has been directed to concentrate on fighting corruption instead of countering terrorism; The Friday Times noted that the IB Chief Dr. Suleman Khan denied this development. Sources within the agency insist that they had been tasked to bring forward corruption cases against prominent political figures and pay attention to these areas. "There are other agencies and organizations which were trained for anti-corruption efforts. IB should not do this. Its expertise is in countering terrorism and its focus should not be redirected towards corruption," said Ehsan Ghani, a recently retired former chief of the IB while talking to TFT. Dr. Suleman, who also served the agency in Khyber Pakhtunkhwa, was counted among those who played a vital role in countering terrorism in the province with the help of the police and the Counter Terrorism Department (CTD). Now, he has agreed to shelve counter-terrorism as a subject of the agency, as another agency has been tasked to deal with it. Dr. Suleman was appointed chief of the agency by former Prime Minister Shahid Khaqan Abbasi on the recommendation of Aftab Sultan, the then IB chief. But Dr Suleman denied this. "I come from a background of counter-terrorism, how I can abandon something I have worked on for years"[13]

The third most important agency-having something on the ball during the Musharaf, Zardari and Nawaz Sharif government is Federal Investigation Agency (FIA). My best friend-Chief of the FIA (Khawar Zaman) once told me the agency had also been playing a political role for different governments since the 1970s. The FIA's main objective is to protect the nation's interests and defend Pakistan, to uphold and enforce law in the country. The Federal Investigation Agency (FIA) was established on 13 January 1975, after being codified in the Constitution with the passing of the FIA Act in 1974. The FIA is headed by the Director-General who is appointed by the Prime Minister, and confirmed by the President. Appointment for the Director of FIA either comes from the high-ranking officials of police or the civil bureaucracy. The DG FIA reports to the Interior Secretary of Pakistan.

The FIA is the biggest intelligence agency in Pakistan. During the last four decades, FIA has been used against alliance-making and punishing political opponents. On 07 October 2020, Newsweek Pakistan reported former Director General of Pakistan's Federal Investigation Agency (FIA), Bashir Memon, summoned by the military establishment and ISI, pushed to register a case against Maryam Nawaz and her husband Muhammad Safdar over a picture of the first lady that was circulated on social media. He told Maiullah Khan that he asked under what law he could register the case. "It was a picture of the first lady on social media. How is this terrorism? There is a definition of terrorism in law. It was a normal picture, how was that terrorism?" he said, adding that this had happened shortly after the 2018 general elections. While refusing to name anyone directly, he stressed that the demand had come from the "highest office" of Pakistan, in a seeming reference to Prime Minister Imran Khan. He, however, said; "[I was told] to take action on this against [Maryam Nawaz's] social media cell. I didn't say this couldn't be done. I just asked under what law? Because we have to work according to the law," he said, adding that the government's expectations of the FIA had since been "fulfilled" by the National Accountability Bureau (NAB"). Memon said. When Mr. Memon was asked to register cases of corruption against them, he replied: "I told them that all of this is the mandate of the provincial anti-corruption [unit]. They can do this, we cannot. Because the FIA is a law enforcement agency.

A law enforcement agency will [handle] law. We will remain within our mandate. We can't go and jump around," he said, adding that he had been criticized for not pursuing such cases against the PMLN. "[P.M. Khan said] 'you didn't do this, you didn't do that, you released that person' and all I said was 'sir NAB is there' [to pursue such cases]," Memon added.

However, Express Tribune reported former Federal Investigation Agency (FIA) Chief Bashir Memon retracted his allegations that Prime Minister Imran Khan had instructed him to initiate a probe against Supreme Court's judge Justice Qazi Faez Isa. In his interview with a private television channel, DG FIA said his meeting with the Prime Minister lasted only for two to three minutes and the premier did not discuss any specific case with him. "The Prime Minister just appreciated my professionalism and told me that being a courageous person, I can do it," he said. Allegations levelled in a TV interview by Bashir Memon were painful. He was, later on called to the Prime Minister's Office for a meeting where the premier told him that he was "a very good officer" who has been registering "good cases" in the past and that he should "take courage" and register a good case this time as well. He said, "At that time, I was not aware of the nature of the case and whom I was supposed to proceed against". Memon claimed that it was at Akbar's office that it was revealed to him that he is to proceed against Justice Qazi Faez Isa

On 24 June 2021, the ISI directed FIA to summon journalist Muhammad Bilal Ghauri for his critical reporting. Thus, Federal Investigation Agency's Cyber Crime Reporting Centre in Islamabad summoned journalist Muhammad Bilal Ghauri for questioning for alleged defamatory remarks made through his YouTube channel. The International Federation of Journalist (IFJ) urged authorities to cease the intimidation of journalists who have a right to freedom of expression and questioning attacks on their profession, but military establishment refused to clear Mr. Ghauri. The summon notice was issued on June 22 under the Pakistan Electronic Crime Act (PECA) and ordered Ghauri to appear before the Cyber Crime Reporting Centre of the Federal Investigation Agency (FIA) in Islamabad. According to a letter from M. Waseem Sikandar, a sub-inspector at the FIA, the summons was in response to a complaint filed by Syed Abbas Mohiuddin, a politician from Attock district and member of the provincial assembly. The letter warned that failing to adhere the notice's order would result in further legal action under section 174 of Pakistan Penal Code.[14]

As I acknowledged earlier, the Federal Investigation Agency was politicized by successive Pakistani governments. Mr. Khawar Zaman, Chief of the

FIA once told this author that Choudhry Shujaat forced him for illegal appointments. FIA has been the source of human trafficking in Europe and South Asia since 1980s. On 28 April, 2021, Pakistan's Supreme Court ordered the FIA to remove the 53-illegally appointed officers. A three-member bench of the apex court headed by Chief Justice of Pakistan Justice Gulzar Ahmed conducted a hearing of a contempt petition against FIA for making unlawful recruitments in the agency and not complying with the Supreme Court order dated 21-02-2001. The FIA counsel informed that four employees have died, while three have passed the competitive exam. He said that after the SC judgment, the FIA employees approached the high courts. Justice Ijaz said that the Supreme Court judgment cannot be overruled by the high courts. Civilian control over intelligence agencies and oversight in Pakistan is a challenging issue. Intelligence agencies in Pakistan operating without oversight became sarcastic.[15] On 04 November 2013, Dawn reported recommendations of the Senate Standing Committee on Human Rights, which "recommended an effective role of parliament in monitoring the Inter-Services Intelligence (ISI) agency and putting it under civilian control. The report was unanimously adopted by the committee and presented in the house. The committee unanimously approved recommendations on 05 September 2013, and voiced for setting up a bicameral intelligence and security committee to suggest ways of addressing the issue of enforced disappearance of citizens".[16]

Chapter 6

Politicians Dancing to the ISI's Jitterbug

The way military intelligence operated over the past decades was not on traditional or cultural patterns, the ISI was dancing to different tangos. Instead of tackling national security challenges, the agency, along with Military Intelligence (MI) and the IB, unnecessarily concentrated on making political alliances and countering democratic forces within the country. When the intelligence war among military and civilian agencies intensified, the blame game became the main focus of literary debates in newspapers and electronic media. Democratic forces stood behind civilian intelligence agencies, while pro-establishment forces supported the ISI and its undemocratic business. In 2014, officials from the ISI had their phone calls eavesdropped on at the height of civil-military tension. On 13 September 2013, Dawn newspaper reported allegations of the Directorate General of Inter-Services Intelligence (ISI) against the 34 civilian inspectors who filed petitions with the Islamabad High Court (IHC) that they were compromising national security and hampered the smooth functioning of the organization as well.[1] In August that year, the ISI inspector Abdul Rahim filed a petition with the IHC saying that contrary to the court restraining orders, the Directorate of ISI had posted him to Sui in Balochistan and also evicted him from the official residence in Islamabad. However, Mr. Justice Shaukat Aziz Siddiqui suspended the posting orders of Mr. Rahim and also restrained the ISI from evicting him from the official residence as well.

Moreover, before this petition, on 01 July 2013, Dawn newspaper reported a petition of the promotion case of civilian officers against the ISI Directorate. The litigation related to the service matter of a number of civilian officials working within offices of Inter-Services Intelligence (ISI) indicated that it was difficult for them to reach even BPS-21-grade in their entire service. Because of this, the names of civilian officials cannot even be considered for the post of Director General which is a BPS-22 position. However, that year, three more petitions were also filed with the Islamabad

High Court (IHC) by the civilian officials of the Inter-Services Intelligence (ISI). All but 30 civilian officials of the ISI Directorates filed their petition against the agency Directorate-stating that a civilian official working in ISI offices hardly gets only one-time promotion during his entire 25 years of service. Reports indicated more than 325 officers were working in BPS-17 to 21 in the five different cadres of the ISI. Out of the 325, only one officer enjoyed BPS-21. Seven others were in BPS-20 and were working as Deputy Directors. Lt-General (retired) Talat Masood said despite being a civilian organization, there was hardly any oversight of the civilian governments over the ISI.[2]

The ISI management has been treating civilian employees like slaves and look at them with scorn. They have no voice, no promotion, and housing rights. One of my close friends-Assistant Director of ISI's Lahore directorate received a single promotion in the past two decades. He is a highly educated officer. Military officers within the agency offices are managing intelligence operations but don't share information with civilian officers. There are countless civilian officers who live hand to mouth as they cannot manage monthly expenditures of their families with a trivial salary they receive, while military officers not only receive huge salaries, but also plundering secret funds in bogus cases. Several disparate civilian friends of this author within the ISI management bawled and yelled before me of their hardship and poverty inflicted by the military management. One of my friends (M) got only one promotion after 23 years, another two left the agency with tears, disposition and protestation. With this culture of militarization and intransigence within the ISI management, the agency lost its professional demonstration in tackling national security challenges. Dawn newspaper on 07 March, 2013, reported contempt petition of civilian employees of ISI and their management and Director General:

"In what may be the first such case in Pakistan's history, four civilian employees of the Inter-Services Intelligence (ISI) have approached the Islamabad High Court (IHC) with complaints about their own chief, ISI Director-General Lt-Gen Zaheerul Islam. They claim that he, along with other senior government officers, should be charged with contempt of court, regarding an IHC ruling on the regularization of employees. The four men, Grade-18 officers, claim to have been working for the past seven years as junior analysts in the ISI, on a contract basis. They claim that their contractual appointments were limited to five years, after which they were to be made permanent employees. Along with other federal government employees, the four officers came to the Islamabad High Court late last year, and on December 31, the IHC directed the government to "regularize the services of contract employees". A cabinet subcommittee supervised the process at various ministries and departments, but these ISI employees were not regularized. The ISI employees have asked the IHC to initiate contempt of court proceedings against Lt-Gen Zaheerul Islam; Lt-Gen (retired) Asif Yasin Malik, Secretary of Defence; Tamiur Azmat Usman, Secretary of the Establishment; and Syed Khursheed Ahmed Shah, chairman of the cabinet subcommittee on regularization of contractual employees. They claim that the respondents did not comply with the IHC's December 31 ruling. An ISI official, however, told Dawn that contract appointments in the ISI are different from those in other departments. "Regular appointments can only be made after candidates complete competitive exams and undergo psychological and intelligence tests," he said. The four petitioners, he claimed, "cannot get permanent positions in the ISI without going through these steps".[3]

The perspicacity that ISI is a number-1 intelligence agency in South Asia is not accurate; the agency is weak, militarized and its national security approach is controversial. It collects intelligence in an untraditional manner, which leads policymakers in the wrong direction. Its intelligence officers are not so greatly educated and unable to use modern intelligence technology properly. There are thousands of volunteer informers who work for the agency in different environments but don't even know the basic knowledge of intelligence information techniques. Their purveyed low-quality intelligence information led policy makers in the wrong direction-the reason that they view Afghanistan and India with hostile military glasses. The second underwhelming thing is that military and civilian officers working within the agency have adopted two cultures of intelligence collection and analysis. In view of the fact that for civilian officers, working in a militarized agency with a military way of operation and administration, is an exasperating task. The ISI collects intelligence information in a militarized manner, analyzes it in a militarized manner, and disseminates it inaccurately.[4] The ISI's operational technique has become militarized. Its civilian approach remained controversial as the agency arrested and disappeared/kidnapped those listed by the establishment.

Pakistan's military establishment and the ISI sponsored terrorism in Afghanistan, committed war crimes and sexually abused women and girls. Ironically, they don't care about women's rights since the Taliban took control of Kabul and imposed its strict restriction on women's activities. Afghans had never thought to go through such a worst scenario ever. A number of annoying news was doing rounds from areas controlled by the Taliban as they did not allow the farmers in Panjwai district of Kandahar to water their grape garden. In the Northern provinces, they torched shops, homes and other public and government institutions. Even the streets were not spared. In Badakhshan, at least 14 districts fell to the Taliban and in neighbouring Takhar province, 15 out of 16 districts were controlled by the Taliban. Pakistani ISI consecutively purveys sophisticated weapons to the Taliban terrorist group to harm national critical infrastructure, undermine Afghan security forces and kill innocent civilians. In Afghanistan, (Pakistan's Inter-Services Intelligence Contributes to Regional Instability. Global Security Review, Alexandra Gilliard-Jun 7, 2019) 'Pakistan's primary goal is to prevent India from gaining ground and obtaining too much influence. As the Taliban vies for more control, the ISI has provided it with military aid to ensure Afghanistan remains in a state of perpetual instability. Should the Taliban gain power, Pakistan will have bought itself a staunch ally in the region, with the potential to form a strategic partnership against India. The ISI killed journalists and political activists in both Afghanistan and Pakistan.[5] John. R. Schmidt (ISI Wrongfully Accused of Killing Journalist?) has highlighted operational mechanism of the ISI:

"But now there are accusations, publicly embraced by U.S. officials (including Joint Chiefs chairman Admiral Mike Mullen), that ISI ordered the murder of Pakistani journalist Saleem Shahzad, whose tortured and severely beaten body was found outside Islamabad on May 31. Shahzad had recently written a piece for the Asia Times alleging that the Pakistani Navy had arrested several naval personnel for helping al-Qaeda attack the Pakistani naval base in Karachi on May 22. Suspicion that ISI may have been responsible for his death surfaced after it was revealed he had earlier told colleagues he had received death threats from the intelligence agency. These threats had allegedly come in the wake of a previous article he had written accusing Pakistani authorities of releasing Afghan Taliban deputy leader Mullah Baradar in October 2010 after eight months in custody. According to Shahzad, senior flag rank ISI officials had pressed him to reveal the source of his information and, when he refused, had made a point of telling him they had recently gotten a hold of an Islamic terrorist hit list and would let him know if his name was on it. Shahzad interpreted this as a threat. The speculation following his death was that the Karachi-naval-base story was the last straw and that ISI had ordered his murder, not just in retaliation, but as a warning to the entire Pakistani journalist community, whose criticisms it believed had gotten out of hand. If ISI was responsible for murdering Shahzad, it may well have been a first.....None of the fifteen fit a plausible ISI scenario. But why would ISI choose Shahzad as its first victim? He was not a big-name journalist, nor was he among those who raised embarrassing questions about ISI and the army over the Abbottabad raid on bin Laden. His Karachi-naval-base story did not accuse ISI of improper conduct, and it is not clear why it would have killed him over a story that, if it embarrassed anyone, would have embarrassed the Pakistani Navy, a relatively minor player in the nation's military firmament. ISI was well aware that some of its senior officers had recently "had a word" with Shahzad and should have realized that if he suddenly turned up murdered ISI might be blamed for it, further sullying its already battered reputation. And that, of course, is exactly what happened".[6]

There are countless cases of corruption within the ISI infrastructure. From weapons smuggling, drug trafficking, human trafficking, sexual abuse, kidnapping, enforced disappearance of political activists, journalists, tribal leaders and land grabbing. The misuse of secret funds leads us to numerous bad news. Digital Desk of Sentinel (19 September 2020) has noted multirole stories of the ISI in Pakistan, and quoted journalist's Declan Walsh book to uncover misgivings of the agency approach to national security and neighbouring states:

"Inter-Services Intelligence, Pakistan's spy agency is afflicted by the same bungling and corruption as the rest of the Pakistani state, according to a new book. The book called, "The Nine Lives of Pakistan", has been authored by Declan Walsh, the Cairo bureau chief of the New York Times. He covered Pakistan for nine years as an international correspondent for The Guardian first and then the Times, before he was expelled from the country. The book points to the fact that ISI uses fear as a weapon but its abilities are often overestimated. "The ISI does little to dispute its reputation as an omnipotent force. Fear is a powerful weapon. But talk of a 'rogue agency' is misplaced, and its abilities are frequently overestimated. While it is effective on street level, and seen by Western spy agencies as superior to its Indian rival, the Research and Analysis Wing (RAW), the ISI is not a professional service in the mould of the CIA or Britain's MI6," according to the book excerpts. "The organization is afflicted by the same bungling and corruption as the rest of the Pakistani state. It has frequently lost control of its most dangerous assets–Puppet masters who can't control their puppets,' as Robert Grenier, a former CIA station chief in Islamabad, put it," the book says. "And when it comes to analysis, the ISI has a poor record. 'They saw everything through pre-determined ideological prisms, rather like the KBG during the Cold War, a senior British official who worked with the ISI for decades told me. 'Frankly,' he added. 'None of their analysis was worth the paper it was written on,'" it adds.[7]

The rivalry between the IB and ISI boiled over in June 2017, when a Joint Investigation Team (JIT) probing alleged money laundering of the Sharif family made a written complaint to the Supreme Court that the IB was wiretapping JIT members, including the ISI and military intelligence personnel. The JIT further reported that the IB was hampering its inquiries, adding that military-led intelligence agencies were not on "good terms" with the IB. More worrisome was that IB was collecting intelligence information on members of the JIT from the National Database and Registration Authority (NADRA) and presented it to Prime Minister Nawaz Sharif to use it against them. The shortcomings of the civilian security apparatus are numerous.[8] Dawn newspaper published an article by journalist Almeida, which said that some in Pakistan's civilian government confronted military officials at a top-secret national security Committee meeting. They said that they were being asked to do more to crack down on armed groups, yet, whenever law-enforcement agencies took action, "the security establishment...worked behind the scenes to set the arrested free". He also reported that the civilians warned that Pakistan risked international isolation if the security establishment didn't crack down on terrorist groups operating from Pakistan. After these leaks, the National Security Council and its committee became controversial. Pakistan's Chief Executive General Pervez Musharraf formally established the National Security Council on 21 August 2002. Under Article 152A of the Pakistan Constitution, the President of Pakistan and the Prime Minister of Pakistan serves as Chairman and Vice Chairman respectively.[9]

The Council remains unpopular and resented by leading political parties and liberal politicians, pointing to the fact that the NSC primarily takes on the oligarchic structure of high-ranking military retirees and elite civilian officials close to the military. The Dawn leak's story uncovered fractured relationship between military establishment and democratic government in Pakistan where the two stakeholders have been trying to push each other to the brink.[10] In a meeting between the army and civilian administration on security issue, Chief Minister warned that the army support to militant organization may possibly exacerbate Pakistan's political and economic challenges in international community. Relations between the army and the Nawaz government were deteriorating by the day, while the ISI and Imran Khan's associates were anxious that the clandestine relationship of Indian RAW and the Sharif family might damage the country's image abroad.

Prime Minister Nawaz Sharif was hopeful that friendly relations between India and Pakistan will bring prosperity to the region, but the armed forces didn't support his line of argument.[11] Express Tribune newspaper (26 April 2017) in its report noted some important points of the leaks argument:

"One member each from the ISI, Military Intelligence and Intelligence Bureau were included in the panel. Establishment Secretary Tahir Shahbaz, Punjab's Ombudsman Najam Saeed and the Federal Investigation Agency Director Usman Anwar were also part of the committee.[12] The committee was assigned the job to establish the identity of those who allegedly planted the story. Former information minister Pervaiz Rashid has already lost his portfolio on the grounds that he failed to play his role effectively to restrain the journalist from running the controversial story". Journalist Cyril Almeida (Exclusive: Act against militants or face international isolation, civilians tell military-DAWN 06 October, 2016), in his story, noted stunning inside fight between the democratic government and military establishment:

"In a blunt, orchestrated and unprecedented warning, the civilian government has informed the military leadership of a growing international isolation of Pakistan and sought consensus on several key actions by the state. As a result of the most recent meeting, an undisclosed one on the day of the All Parties' Conference on Monday, at least two sets of actions have been agreed. First, ISI DG Gen Rizwan Akhtar, accompanied by National Security Adviser Nasser Janjua, is to travel to each of the four provinces with a message for provincial apex committees and ISI sector commanders. The message: military-led intelligence agencies are not to interfere if law enforcement acts against militant groups that are banned or until now considered off-limits for civilian action. Gen Akhtar's inter-provincial tour began with a visit to Lahore. Second, Prime Minister Nawaz Sharif has directed that fresh attempts be made to conclude the Pathankot investigation and restart the stalled Mumbai attacks-related trials in a Rawalpindi anti-terrorism court. Those decisions, taken after an extraordinary verbal confrontation between Punjab Chief Minister Shahbaz Sharif and the ISI DG, appear to indicate a high-stakes new approach by the PML-N government........The foreign secretary's unexpectedly blunt conclusions triggered an astonishing and potentially ground-shifting exchange between the ISI DG and several civilian officials. In response to Foreign Secretary Chaudhry's conclusions, Gen Akhtar asked what steps could be taken to prevent the drift towards isolation. Mr Chaudhry's reply was direct and emphatic: the principal international demands are for action against Masood Azhar and the Jaish-i-Mohmmad; Hafiz Saeed and the Lashkar-e-Taiba; and the Haqqani network. To that, Gen Akhtar offered that the government should arrest whomever it deems necessary, though it is unclear whether he was referring to particular individuals or members of banned groups generally. At that point came the stunning and unexpectedly bold intervention by Punjab Chief Minister Shahbaz Sharif....Earlier in the meeting, ISI DG Gen Akhtar stated that not only is it the military's policy to not distinguish between militant groups, but that the military is committed to that policy prevailing. The ISI chief did mention concerns about the timing of action against several groups, citing the need to not be seen as buckling to Indian pressure or abandoning the Kashmiri people".[13]

Moreover, Daily Dawn reported on the military establishment's standpoint of leaks on 14 October 2016. Participants of a Corps Commanders meeting at General Headquarters in Rawalpindi expressed serious concern over what they said was a leak from a security meeting which was reported by Dawn earlier this month. In a statement issued by Inter-Services Public Relations (ISPR), participants of the meeting expressed serious concern over "feeding of a false and fabricated story of an important security meeting held at PM House and viewed it as a breach of national security." Chief of Army Staff (COAS) General Raheel Sharif presided over the meeting which was attended by all corps commanders and principal staff officers. Almeida's name was added to the Exit Control List–preventing travel abroad – on Monday after he wrote the news report "Act against militants or face international isolation, civilians tell military." The Prime Minister's Office rejected the story thrice since it was published on October 6.[14] In an Editor's note, Dawn clarified its position and stated on the record that the story "was verified, cross-checked and fact-checked." The note further stated: "Many at the helm of affairs are aware of the senior officials and participants of the meeting who were contacted by the newspaper for collecting information. Therefore, the elected government and state institutions should refrain from targeting the messenger and scapegoating the country's most respected newspaper in a malicious campaign." In the wake of the travel ban on Almeida, human rights and journalists' organizations including the HRCP, PFUJ and CPNE protested and rallied in his support. Most TV news channels also ran reports and conducted programes criticizing the government's decision. The newspaper reported. Moreover, on 12 October 2016, DAWN newspaper reported the fallout of the story:

"The fallout of the story has been intense, and on Tuesday evening, the government placed Dawn's senior writer, Cyril Almeida, on the Exit Control List. While any media organization can commit an error of judgement and Dawn is no exception, the paper believes it handled the story in a professional manner and carried it only after verification from multiple sources. Moreover, in accordance with the principles of fair and balanced journalism, for which Dawn is respected not only in Pakistan but also internationally, it twice carried the denials issued by the Prime Minister's Office. Journalism has a long and glorious tradition of keeping its promise to its audience even in the face of enormous pressure brought to bear upon it from the corridors of power. Time has proved this to be the correct stance. Some of the most contentious yet historically significant stories have been told by news organizations while resisting the state's narrow, self-serving and ever-shifting definition of 'national interest'. One could include in this list, among others, the Pentagon Papers detailing US government duplicity in its conduct of the Vietnam War; the Abu Ghraib pictures that exposed torture of prisoners at the hands of US soldiers in Iraq; the WikiLeaks release in 2010 of US State Department diplomatic communications; and Edward Snowden's disclosure of the National Security Agency's global surveillance system. Even more so in Pakistan, where decades of a militarized security environment have undermined the importance of holding the state to account — something that certain sections of the media have become complicit in despite their long, hard-won struggle for freedom — such a furor as generated by the Dawn report was not unexpected." Dawn noted.[15]

The Almeida report found Prime Minister guilty. On 20 April 2017, Press Trust of India reported proxy war between the government and armed forces, and noted removal of Tariq Fatemi, advisor to the Prime Minister after an inquiry found him guilty of "leaking" to a prominent newspaper vital information from a high-level National Security meeting. In October 2016, a columnist for Dawn newspaper, Cyril Almeida, wrote a front-page story about a rift between Pakistan's civilian and military leaderships over militant groups that operate from Pakistan but engage in proxy war against India and Afghanistan. The government had set up the inquiry committee to probe the controversy surrounding a controversial report by Dawn newspaper about a key meeting on national security. According to the inquiry committee report, it was Fatemi who was primarily responsible for leaking a report of the key meeting to the newspaper without due permission. Press Trust of India noted.[16] On 10 June 2017, The Wire reported the explosive news story with anonymous sources about a confrontation between Pakistan's Prime Minister and the country's top intelligence chief resulted in several government officials losing their jobs and a newspaper being intimidated, revealing Pakistani state and military officials' limited regard for press freedom......Pakistan's interior ministry first denied the story and put Almeida on the Exit Control List (ECL), an extraordinary measure usually reserved for hardened criminals or people involved in mass fraud and corruption. When Almeida's publication stood by him and refused to reveal its source, the government was forced to remove Almeida from the ECL and launched its own investigation into the source of the leak.[17]

On April 29, General Asif Ghafoor, the spokesman for the Inter-Services Public Relations (ISPR) expressed his institution's dissatisfaction over the government's probe into the leak that put the military and the civilian government on a collision course. "Notification on Dawn Leak is incomplete and not in line with recommendations by the Inquiry Board. "Notification is rejected," Ghafoor said on Twitter. When Ghafoor was writing this tweet, he probably had no idea it would anger a large number of people in Pakistan. Journalist Almeida's story came out at a particularly sensitive time for Islamabad, as its ties with New Delhi deteriorated following tensions on the Kashmir border. Indian Prime Minister Narendra Modi vowed in a speech that he would work to isolate Pakistan internationally due to its alleged support to Islamic militants in Kashmir. Pakistani establishment never allowed controlling the hydra of intelligence agencies to introduce security sector reforms, and fit it to the fight against radicalization, terrorism and jihadism. Consequently, the ISI strategies became militarized and became a tool of miltablishment to harass politicians and those who write against the corruption of military Generals. Scholar Frederic Grare (18 December 2015) noted some aspects of the business of military establishment in his well-written paper:

"Despite more than eight years of continued civilian power, Pakistan can be labelled as a transitional democracy at best. True, the country has experienced two successive and relatively democratic elections in February 2008 and May 2013, and the mainstream political parties--essentially the Pakistan Muslim League Nawaz faction (PML-N) and the Pakistan People's Party (PPP)--are no longer willing to let themselves be played off the other by the military, thereby limiting the margin of manoeuvre of the security establishment. Today, as much as in the past, "operations against dissenting politicians, objective intellectuals, and other activists are still carried out through systematic harassment, disinformation campaigns, fictitious trials, kidnap, torture, and assassinations", as demonstrated by the de facto genocide in Baluchistan."[18]

The continuous militarization and Talibanisation of society, and instability led to the catastrophe of disintegration and failure of the state, which was further inflamed by the US so-called war on terrorism, and the involvement of NATO forces in Afghanistan. Pakistan's weak and unprofessional diplomatic approach towards Afghanistan prompted a deep crisis, including the closure of trade routes and a diplomatic impasse. According to the Constitution of Pakistan, every democratic government is answerable to the people of Pakistan. But in reality, they are actually answerable to the Army headquarters in Rawalpindi. Every single Prime Minister in Pakistan can only do his or her job smoothly if they completely surrender defence, interior, strategic decisions and foreign policy to the Army. It means the rules for civilian governments are pre-decided and they have been told to go by the book and not cross the red-lines defined by the defence establishment. This makes it a "State within a State " that, instead of ruling the country from the front, prefers that the politicians and civilian governments implement their decisions and exercise power. On 22 September 2015, I put in writing that radicalized elements within the army can facilitate the access of Taliban, ISIS and Lashkar-e-Toiba to steal material from dirty bombs. My predictions became a reality when military intelligence and ISI arrested Dr. Wasim Akram and Brigadier Raja Rizwan (retd), who the ISPR described as an employee of a "sensitive organization. Dr. Wasm was working as a nuclear scientist at the Kahuta Nuclear Research Labs, Pakistan's main uranium enrichment facility.[19]

Over the last two decades, the role and scale of Pakistan's intelligence agencies has grown over and above their prescribed functions, to the degree that their operations, often undercover and at odds even with each other, have earned them the repute of being a "State within a State ". In most parts of the country, intelligence information collection faces numerous difficulties since the Taliban and other militant groups returned to important strategic locations. Having faced serious difficulties in dealing with insurgent forces in Balochistan and Waziristan, the agencies started translating their anger into the killing and kidnapping of innocent civilians with impunity. They needed to adopt a professional mechanism in countering insurgency in Waziristan. The way intelligence operated over the past decades was not based on traditional or cultural patterns. Instead of tackling national security challenges, the ISI, along with Military

Intelligence (MI) and other units, mostly concentrated on countering democratic forces within the country[20]

On 06 October 2016, Dawn newspaper reported an unprecedented warning of civilian government to the military leadership of a growing international isolation of Pakistan and sought consensus on several key actions by the state. First, DG of ISI Gen Rizwan Akhtar, accompanied by National Security Adviser General Nasser Janjua, was instructed to travel the four provinces with a message for provincial apex committees and ISI sector commanders. The message warned that military-led intelligence agencies must not interfere when law enforcement acts against militant groups that were banned or until now considered off-limits for civilian action. Second, former Prime Minister Nawaz Sharif directed that fresh attempts be made to conclude the Pathankot investigation and restart the stalled Mumbai attacks-related trials in a Rawalpindi anti-terrorism court. Those decisions, taken after an extraordinary verbal confrontation between Punjab Chief Minister Shahbaz Sharif and the DG ISI, appeared to indicate a high-stakes new approach by the PML-N government. However, during the meeting, Gen Akhtar offered that the government should arrest whomever it deems necessary, but Shahbaz Sharif told Gen Akhtar that when action is taken against certain groups by civilian authorities, military intelligence worked behind the scene to set the arrested free. Dawn reported.[21]

In July 2019, Prime Minister Imran Khan on his official visit to the United States admitted the presence of 30000-40000 armed terrorists in his country. The agencies established links with fundamentalist parties such as the Jamaat-e-Islami and its offshoots, the Tablighi Jamaat and Markaz Dawa-al Irshad. This interaction also allowed the Islamic fundamentalist parties in Pakistan to extend influence over armed forces personnel. The U.S. Country Reports on Terrorism described Pakistan as a "Terrorist safe haven" where terrorists are able to organize, plan, raise funds, communicate, and recruit fighters, while the ISI, has often been accused of playing a role in major terrorist attacks across India including terrorism in Kashmir. President Hamid Karzai was regularly reiterating allegations that militants operating training camps in Pakistan used it as a launch platform to attack targets in Afghanistan. Pakistan's relations with Afghanistan have been in strain due to the former Chief Executive General Musharaf's short-sighted policies. The General shamelessly genuflected to the United States demands of it's so called war on terrorism and accepted all terms and conditions of allowing US and NATO forces to bomb Afghanistan from their bases inside Pakistan. By virtue of Musharraf's short-sighted policies,

Pakistan was pushed into the Afghan quagmire. Pervez Musharraf came under instant U.S. and NATO pressure to act against Al-Qaeda leader Osama bin Laden, who was hiding in Pakistan. In an interview aired by a private channel in 2018, Mr. Musharraf acknowledged that terrorists were trained in Pakistan. "We trained the Taliban and sent them to fight against Russia. Taliban, Haqqani, Osama bin Laden and Zawahiri were our heroes then," he said.

The arrest of Afghan Ambassador Mullah Abdul Salam Zaeef by the ISI military units further caused misunderstanding between the people of Afghanistan and Pakistan. The ISI committed war crimes in Afghanistan and Waziristan. Former Afghan Ambassador Mullah Zaeef was arrested and handed over to US agencies by Pakistani ISI. He was humiliated by the CIA in the presence of ISI in Islamabad. John F. Burns 04 January 2002) published a detailed story of his humiliation and torture in New York Times. Pakistani analyst Ayaz Amir (daily Dawn. 22 September 2006) also noted some aspects of his painful instant:

"We know, to our lasting shame, how our overlords, dazzled by American power, and afraid of God knows what, handed over the ex-Taliban ambassador, Mullah Abdus Salam Zaeef, to the Americans in January 2002—in violation of every last comma of international law. But until now, we have not been privy to the details: how exactly did the handing-over take place? Now to satisfy our curiosity, and perhaps outrage our feelings, comes Mullah Zaeef's own account, published in Pashto and parts of which have been translated into Urdu by the Express newspaper. To say that the account is eye-opening would be an understatement. It is harrowing and mind-blowing. Can anyone bend so low as our government did? And can behaviour be as wretched as that displayed by American military personnel into whose custody Zaeef was given? On the morning of 02 January, 2002, three officials of a secret agency arrived at Zaeef's house in Islamabad with this message: "Your Excellency, you are no more excellency." One of them said no one can resist American power or words to that effect. "America wants to question you. We are going to hand you over to the Americans so that their purpose is served and Pakistan is saved from a big danger." Zaeef could have been forgiven for feeling stunned. From the "guardians of Islam" this was the last thing that he expected, that for the sake of a few "coins" (his words) he would be delivered as a "gift" to the Americans. Under heavy escort he was taken to Peshawar, kept there for a few days and then pushed into his nightmare. Blindfolded and handcuffed, he was driven to a place where a helicopter was waiting, its engines running. Someone said, "Khuda hafiz" (God preserve you).[22]

Ayaz Amir also reported his painful journey, and noted Pakistan's constraints as well. This was Pakistan's bigger mistake that changed the attitude of every Afghan about the country. Mullah Abdul Salam Zaeef, the Taliban Government's Ambassador to Pakistan, in his book "My Life with the Taliban", has described his heartbreaking story: "When we arrived in Peshawar, I was taken to a lavishly-fitted office. A Pakistani flag stood on the desk, and a picture of Mohammad Ali Jinnah hung at the back of the room. A Pashtun man was sitting behind the desk. He got up, introduced himself and welcomed me. His head was shaved — seemingly his only feature of note — and he was of an average size and weight. He walked over to me and said that he was the head of the bureau. I was in the devil's workshop, the regional head office of the ISI. He told me I was a close friend —a guest —and one that they cared about a great deal. I wasn't really sure what he meant since it was pretty clear that I was dear to them only because they could get a good sum of money for me when they sold me. Their trade was people; just as with goats, the higher the price for the goat, the happier the owner. In the twenty-first century, there aren't many places left where you can still buy and sell people, but Pakistan remains a hub for this trade. I prayed after dinner with the ISI officer, and then was brought to a holding-cell for detainees.........Finally, after days in my cell; a man came, tears flowing down his cheeks. He fainted as his grief and shame overcame him. He was the last person I saw in that room. I never learnt his name, but soon after—perhaps four hours after he left — I was handed over to the Americans. Even before I reached the helicopter, I was suddenly attacked from all sides. People kicked me, shouted at me, and my clothes were cut with knives. They ripped the black cloth from my face and for the first time I could see where I was. Pakistani and American soldiers stood around me. The Pakistani soldiers were all staring as the Americans hit me and tore the remaining clothes off my body. Eventually, I was completely naked, and the Pakistani soldiers—the defenders of the Holy Qur'an—shamelessly watched me with smiles on their faces, saluting this disgraceful action of the Americans".[23]

The ISI established relationships with numerous groups and political organizations in Afghanistan, but it's persisting policy inside the country causes distrust. The ISI wants Indian intelligence to curtail its presence in Afghanistan but doesn't want to undermine its own networks. The ISI never tolerated the Indian RAW presence in Afghanistan, the reason that its role in managing several anti-India proxy networks was also unmistakable. On 07 May 2018; Javid Ahmad in his article, revealed so many new things about the ISI role in Afghanistan: "In Afghanistan, ISI's Afghan operations are undertaken by at least three units. The first is Directorate S, the principal covert action arm that directs and oversees the Afghan policy, including militant and terrorist outfits and their operations. The second unit is the Special Service Group (SSG), also known as the Pakistani SS, and is the army's Special Forces element that was established in the 1950s as a hedge against the communists. Today, some SSG units effectively operate as ISI's paramilitary wing and have fought alongside the Taliban until 2001. In other instances, SSG advisors have allegedly been embedded with Taliban fighters to provide tactical military advice, including on special operations, surveillance, and reconnaissance. In fact, encountering ISI operatives fighting alongside the Taliban in Afghanistan has become a common occurrence that no longer surprises Afghan and American forces. The third ISI unit is the Afghan Logistics Cell, a transport network inside Pakistan facilitated by members of Pakistan's Frontier Corps that provide logistical support to the Taliban and their families. This includes space, weapons, vehicles, protection, money, identity cards and safe passage. Such ISI support networks have been designed to break Afghanistan into pieces and then remould it into a pliant state. The objective is to complicate Afghanistan's security landscape and drive its political climate into uncharted constitutional territory to create a vacuum, which inevitably places the Taliban in the driving seat. These support actions have visibly made the group more effective. However, the Pakistani mantra is that they maintain contacts with the Taliban but exercise no control over them".[24]

Chapter 7

War Criminals and Pilferers

On 13 August 2020, Ehsanullah Ehsan revealed that Pakistani authorities had given him a hit list of people who they would like to be killed in Khyber Pakhtunkhwa.[1] In audio, he claimed that after some time of his surrender, he was given the list of prominent voices in order to facilitate Pakistan in eliminating rogue elements. Daily Times reported his confession audio, in which he admitted: "I was asked to lead a death squad and accept killing of the listed people from Khyber Pakhtunkhwa and Pashtuns from all walks of life including journalists.[2] In the audio, he talked about his conversations with ISI and the parleys that took place.[3] Ehsanullah Ehsan (Liaqat Ali) was a former spokesman of Tehreek-e-Taliban Pakistan (TTP) and Jamaat-ul-Ahrar.[4]In April 2017, Inter-Services Public Relations (ISPR) Director-General Asif Ghafoor announced that Ehsan had surrendered himself to Pakistan's security agencies· In early February 2020, Ehsanullah claimed that escaped from the custody of Pakistani Agencies.[5] Journalist and Analyst, Kunwar Khuldune Shahid (The diplomat--April 20, 2020) documented important aspects of Ehsanullah Ehsan's mission:

"Military officials have claimed that Ehsan was an important counterterror asset who had been helping the military take down TTP hideouts across the country, especially in the former tribal areas along the Afghanistan border. The military and government officials have refused to comment on Ehsan, only confirming his escape initially, while claiming that "a lot" is being done in its aftermath. The Army aired Ehsan's confessional statement in April 2017, which was followed by an interview with Pakistan's top media house. However, the Geo TV interview was blocked from being aired by the Pakistan Electronic Media Regulatory Authority (PEMRA) over "glorification of a terrorist." The aired trailer of the interview was deemed insensitive by many, given that the interviewee had taken responsibility for the killings of thousands of Pakistanis. The attacks Ehsan owned on behalf of the TTP and JA included bombings targeting religious minorities and marginalized Islamic sects. Among the most high-profile attacks claimed by Ehsan on behalf of the Taliban was the one aimed at now Nobel Laureate and education activist Malala Yousafzai in October 2012…….Ehsan recalls that many in the TTP and JA had left to join IS when the group first began to expand from the Middle East to South Asia. That resulted in multiple attacks across Pakistan being simultaneously claimed by the Taliban and the Islamic State. The former Taliban spokesman, however, believes that following the February deal with the United States, it is the Afghan Taliban who hold the most clout in the region as far as the militant outfits are concerned".[6]

The Sunday Guardian (06 September 2020) reported Mr. Ehsanullah Ehsan conversation with Taliban leader Mullah Wali-ur-Rahman about the secret mission of their fighters and suicide bombers: "Maulana Wali-ur-Rehman took a letter out of the envelope and gave it to me and told me to read it. I opened the letter and read it aloud. After doing so, Maulana Wali-ur-Rehman said to me, "You must have known why you were called in an emergency for this meeting." I smiled and said, "Yes, I know." The letter I read was written by the DG ISI, General Shuja Pasha to Maulana Wali-ur-Rehman Mehsud. In it, General Shuja Pasha made an offer to the TTP leadership that if the TTP gave up its armed struggle against Pakistan, the ISI would not only provide them with a safe passage against NATO forces in Afghanistan but also provide financial and military support in every possible way. In this letter, General Shuja Pasha also praised the strength and capabilities of the TTP and called the TTP a necessity for Pakistan.[7]

He wrote that we should work together to remove the misunderstandings between the Pakistan army and the TTP and work together to drive the great enemy US (America) and NATO out of Afghanistan. General Pasha had also written that if TTP accepted the demands, the TTP would not just be able to demonstrate its abilities in Waziristan but the whole of Pakistan would be open for the TTP and that the cadre of TTP and their children would be able to work in this country by getting education from educational institutions in Islamabad and Peshawar……In this detailed letter, General Shuja Pasha had repeatedly referred to the Indian "occupation" of and "atrocities" in Kashmir. He had written to Maulana Wali-ur-Rehman Sahib saying that his forefathers had fought many wars for the independence of Kashmir and had made many sacrifices because they were true and patriotic Pakistanis. He, in the letter, had added that he should also join the Pakistan army in the "Ghazwa-e-Hind" war against India, because the war against India is a true and just jihad against the real infidels and polytheists. He also mentioned some Pakistan-backed organizations (Lashker-e-Tayyaba and Jaish-e-Mohammad) who were fighting against India in Kashmir and said that despite all the international pressure, the Pakistan army was helping them because they were fighting for Pakistan.[8]

Professor of American University, Stephen Tankel, (Domestic Barriers to Dismantling the Militant Infrastructure in Pakistan, September 2013), in his research paper, documented Pakistan's sponsorship of Taliban and Sectarian terrorists groups and noted how the ISI used these groups against India and Afghanistan. He also noted that by supporting the US war on terrorism in Afghanistan, the ISI established links with Al Qaeda and Taliban to destabilize the Karzai government. General Musharaf admitted in his interview with the Guardian newspaper (February 2015) that due to Karzai's close relationship with India, he had ordered the ISI to target his government institutions. Pakistan's sponsorship of terrorism in Afghanistan and India is not a new thing, its sponsorship of sectarian groups inside Afghanistan received worldwide criticism:

"Pakistan played host to numerous militant groups during the 1990s. One way to understand the militant milieu at that time is to consider sectarian affiliation. Most groups belong to the Deobandi sect, which follows the Hanafi School of Islamic jurisprudence. The major groups emerged from or were tied to the Deobandi Jamiat Ulema-e-Islam (Assembly of Islamic Clergy, or JUI) as well as the robust madrassa (religious school) system associated with it. The largest and most notable of them included: Harkat-ul-Jihad-al-Islami (HuJI); Harkat-ul-Mujahideen (HuM), which splintered from HuJI, Jaish-e-Mohammed (JeM), which broke from HuM, Sipah-e-Sahaba Pakistan (SSP), and Lashkar-e-Jhangvi (LeJ), which initially formed as the militant wing of SSP before nominally splitting from it. Separately, Lashkar-e-Taiba (LeT) was the biggest and most significant group to emerge from the Ahl-e-Hadith movement, which is Salafi st in orientation. Strong divisions existed between LeT and the Deobandi outfit. Collectively, these entities are known as Punjabi militant groups, a moniker that derives from their being headquartered, and having their strongest support base, in Punjab, Pakistan's most populated and powerful province. Elsewhere, Tehreek-e-Nafaz-e-Shariat-e-Mohammadi (TNSM), formed by a dissident member of Jamaat-e-Islami named Sufi Muhammad in 1989, was based in Malakand and had a blend of Deobandi and Wahhabi leanings. Domestic Barriers to Dismantling the Militant Infrastructure in Pakistan Another way of understanding the militant milieu at the time is to consider activities by location. In addition to indigenous Kashmiri groups, during the 1990s the Pakistani security apparatus also backed a welter of Pakistani groups against Indian security forces in Indian-administered Kashmir. These included the Deobandi HuM, HuJI, and JeM, as well as the Ahl-e-Hadith LeT".[9]

M. Ilyas Khan (Uncovering Pakistan's secret human rights abuses, BBC News, Dera Ismaìl Khan, 02 June 2019), in his commentary on BBC website documented atrocities of Pakistan army in North Waziristan: "In May 2016, for example, an attack on a military post in the Teti Madakhel area of North Waziristan triggered a manhunt by troops who rounded up the entire population of a village. An eyewitness who watched the operation from wheat field nearby and whose brother was among those detained told the BBC that the soldiers beat everyone with batons and threw mud in children's mouths when they cried. A pregnant woman was one of two people who died during torture, her son said in video testimony. At least one man remains missing. Local activists say more than 8,000 people picked up by the army since 2002 remain unaccounted for".[10]

General Hamid Gul was a defence analyst and Chief of ISI during the Zia regime (1987-1989). He was the architect of Afghan jihad and father of Afghan Taliban. He was a supporter of Kashmiri Mujahideen, Chechen, Uighurs and Bosnian Mujahideen. In 1988, with the support of Osama Bin Laden, he formed Islamic Jamhoori Ittihad against the Pakistan People Party. On 15 August 2015, he died of brain haemorrhage in Murry. On 12 March 2007, Gul marched alongside activists from the liberal democratic parties and retired former senior military officers against General Pervez Musharraf. In 2007, Benazir Bhutto wrote to General Musharaf about the involvement of General Hamid Gul, Chief of Intelligence Bureau (IB) Brigadier Ijaz Shah, the then Chief Minister of Punjab Chaudhry Pervaiz Elahi, then Chief Minister of Sindh Arbab Ghulam Rahim, in the terrorist attacks in Karachi. However, he was placed on US Global Terrorism list in 2008.

On 16 August 2015, DW news quoted a Pakistan's news channel indication that Hamid Gul was not dead; he was alive in the form of numerous jihadist organizations, including the Taliban, and in the Islamist narratives of the Pakistani state that have persisted since the 1980s Afghan War. Gul's role in spearheading an Islamist insurgency in Indian-administered Kashmir is also well-documented. New Delhi holds him responsible for diverting militants and arms from the Afghan war to Srinagar toward the end of his job as spy chief in 1989. India and Pakistan have fought two wars over Kashmir since their independence from Britain in 1947. Following his retirement,

Gul became a security expert and could be seen on television defending both the Taliban and Kashmiri militants. He was frequently invited by the Islamist parties to their anti-West rallies. DW news reported.[11] Moreover on 15 August 2015, BBC reported critics describing him as a delusional conspiracy theorist who had little regard for democratic politics, hard-liner supporters considered him a patriotic Pakistani:

"A self-styled master strategist, Gen Gul spent much of his time since retiring as a pundit propounding various conspiracy theories. Once a close ally of the American CIA, he became passionately anti-US. After the 11 September attacks, he was seen as a prominent apologist for Osama Bin Laden and jihadi groups. He was seen as a hero by pro-army, right-wing clerics and politicians. His critics say he reflected an aggressive and often delusional military mindset. Gen Gul derived much of his significance from his brief two-year stint as director-general of the ISI. The late eighties were a crucial time in the region. The Afghan war against the Soviets was coming to an end and the Kashmiri insurgency against India was starting. In Pakistan, Gen Gul's mentor President General Zia ul-Haq died in a mysterious plane crash in August 1988, paving the way for first party-based national polls in eleven years. As Pakistan's chief spymaster, Gen Gul played a key role in influencing and shaping those events. His supporters credit him with diverting fighters, funds and guns from the Afghan Jihad to the Kashmir front. At home, he was accused of rigging the 1988 election by propping up a hardline Islamist alliance to prevent Benazir Bhutto from coming into power". BBC reported.[12]

Analyst Shekhar Gupta (25 May 2018) expressed his love for anti-India elements in 1987 when Zia-ul-Haq named him as Chief of ISI. After Zia's death, Bhutto detested him as much as he hated her. The previous year, he had masterminded the raising of Islamic Jamhoori Ittihad (IJI) to keep her out of power. But even now, he was too powerful for her to remove as ISI chief. That opportunity came the following year. With Zia gone, and the new chief of the army staff (Mirza Aslam Beg) way more reckless and stupid, Gul had a free run. For the first time, he threw the might of Pakistani army regulars to fight alongside the Mujahedeen and defeat the army of Najibullah after the Soviet withdrawal. This was a disaster. Mr. Shekhar noted. One more personality of the same valour and resilience was General Javed Nasir, Director General of the Inter-Services Intelligence (ISI), and an active member of Tablighi Jamaat in Raiwind Lahore, where he had established different intelligence unites for intelligence information collection from different parts of Pakistan. He used Tablighi Jamaat as an international spy campaign across the world. In the military circles, Maj-Gen. Nasir was described as a "moderate person" who rediscovered the Islam in 1986 during the midst of the Russian war in neighbouring Afghanistan. In 1989, he was appointed as Director General of Frontier Works Organization (FWO).[13]

On 14 March 1992, Prime Minister Nawaz Sharif appointed Lt-Gen Nasir as the Director-General of the Inter-Services Intelligence (ISI) against the recommendations and wishes of General Asif Nawaz, then-Chief of Army Staff. In April 1992, Lt-Gen. Nasir became an international figure when he played a major role in amalgamating the scattered Afghan mujahedeen groups when the power-sharing formula was drafted. He also trained Afghan and Pakistani Mujahideen and sent them for fights against the Serbian army in Bosnia. From Jalalabad Airport, the Pakistan army and the ISI were transporting Afghans to Bosnia. In 1992–93, Nasir defied the UN arms embargo placed on Bosnia and Herzegovina when he successfully airlifted the POF's sophisticated anti-tank guided missiles, which ultimately turned the tide in favour of Bosnian Muslims and forced the Serbs to life the siege much to the annoyance of the U.S. government. In 2011, the International Criminal Tribunal for the former Yugoslavia demanded the custody of the former ISI director for his alleged support of the Inter-Services Intelligence activities in Bosnia and Herzegovina to Muslim fighters of Bosnia against the Serbian army in the 1990s, the Government of Pakistan refused to hand Nasir to the UN tribunal, citing poor health. The ISI role in Bosnia, Afghanistan and India is seen by military and intelligence experts a destructive and shameful.[14]

Pakistan Press International on 15 May 2005, reported the PPP reference against the ISI DG Lieutenant General Javed Nasir for financial bungling and compromising national secrets, with the National Accountability Bureau (NAB). Through its counsel Shah Khawar, the PPP asked Chairman of the NAB to investigate press reports Javed Nasir' involvement in the defalcation of bank loans, committed financial irregularities and compromised national secrets. PPI noted. However, Pakistan Press International noted his involvement in loan default and other cases. The PPP contended that the ex-ISI chief was investigated for unpaid loans and alleged involvement in drugs by the NAB, but the investigations were halted by the government. PPI noted.[15]

The Kargil crisis was initiated by the ISI and General Musharaf in 1999. G Parthasarathy (Rogue army runs the show-11 January 2003, The Pioneer) noted some aspects of the ISI role in conflicts in South Asia: "Despite protestations of innocence by General Musharraf, the ISI still deals with these parties more or less as natural allies. After ousting Ms. In 1991, the army funded the opposition alliance that brought Mr. Nawaz Sharif to power. Mr Sharif himself entered politics as a protégé of General Zia..... The role of the ISI in spreading Islamist terror across the globe has come into sharper focus since the commencement of America's war on terrorism. Despite denials, it is now established that the ISI sent senior officers, soldiers and ex-servicemen to sustain and fight alongside the Taliban regime. The ISI also actively connived with the Taliban in supporting terrorist groups ranging from the Chechens to the Islamic Movement of Uzbekistan in Central Asia and Abu Sayyaf in the Philippines. Former ISI Chief General Javed Nasir has now revealed that the Americans had sought his ouster in 1993 because he secretly arranged for the airlift of anti-tank missiles and other weaponry to Bosnian Muslims in violation of United Nations sanctions".[16]

Director-General of the Inter-Services Intelligence (ISI), retired Lt Gen Zaheerul Islam, was involved in politics by supporting Imran Khan against Nawaz Sharif. "I was told to step down and go home. I said whatever you want to do, do it. I will not resign from the prime minister's office," Nawaz Sharif said. Later on, he constituted a coup against Nawaz Sharif. In a detailed commentary on the involvement of ISI in the PTI Dharna, The Herald Magazine, on 06 October 2015, noted: "There were rumours in the air. During the 126-day-long dharna by Pakistan Tehreek-e-Insaf (PTI) against the ruling Pakistan Muslim League–Nawaz (PMLN), there were murmurs of a coup d'état. Other than General Shuja Pasha, the former intelligence officer who is known to be a close friend and supporter of PTI Chairman Imran Khan, the other name that was repeatedly brought up was that of Zaheerul Islam, the then director general of the Inter-Services Intelligence (ISI). Allegedly, the two were conspiring to create a rift between Prime Minister Nawaz Sharif and Chief of Army Staff General Raheel Sharif. In the past, the premier had acted against generals whom he had differences with. It was expected that he would again act in a similar manner, under the presumption that the dharna had the general's backing. But the events did not play out as expected. Not exactly......Not everyone took from his experience. In an interview with the BBC in August 2015, Senator Mushahidullah Khan claimed that an audio tape obtained by the Intelligence Bureau was played during a meeting between Prime Minister Nawaz Sharif and Raheel Sharif in 2017, in which Islam could be heard giving instructions to raid the prime minister's office. According to the senator, when questioned by General Raheel Sharif, Islam confirmed that the voice was his own. Khan later clarified that he himself had not heard the tape. Never mind the fact that he kept referring to the ex-ISI Chief as Zahirul Islam Abbasi – the major general who had plotted to overthrow the Benazir Bhutto government in 1995, and who died six years ago – the damage had been done".[17]

General Javed Nasir and General Zaheerul Islam have been dancing to different tangos since 1990s. Journalist Saleem Shahzad (Cracking open Pakistan's jihadi core Posted in Broader Middle East, 19-Aug-04, Asia Times) in his article uncovered suspicious activities of the jihadist core of Pakistan army, and its affiliation with jihadist terrorist organizations. He also unmasked the jihadist core support to Lashkar-e-Toiba and other extremist groups that fought jihad in Kashmir and Afghanistan:

"The recent arrest of two top Pakistani jihadis, Maulana Fazalur Rehman Khalil and Qari Saifullah Akhtar, marks the beginning of the end of an era that started in the mid-1980s when the dream of an International Muslim Brigade was first conceived by a group of top Pakistan leaders. The dream subsequently materialized in the shape of the International Islamic Front, an umbrella organization for militant groups formed by Osama bin Laden in 1998 and loosely coordinated by the Lashkar-e-Toiba (LET) of Pakistan. The arrests in Pakistan, made under relentless pressure from the United States, are aimed at tracing all jihadi links to their roots, which are mostly grounded in Pakistan's strategic core. As a former Pakistan Inter-Services Intelligence (ISI) operator and air force official, Khalid Khawaja, commented in the Pakistani press on the arrests of the two jihadis, "Every link of the arrested jihadi leaders goes straight to top army officials of different times. To keep the Arab movements under control, an al-Badr facility was organized in Khost province in Afghanistan. A dynamic law and master of arts graduate from Karachi University, Bakhat Zameen Khan, a member of the Jamaat-i-Islami (JI), a powerful religious party (who originally hailed from Dir in North West Frontier Province), was chosen as commander. He brought together all Arab jihadis at the facility, and linked senior ones to the ISI. Out of this camp, the Palestinian Hamas emerged, as well as the Arab-sponsored Moro liberation movement led by Abu Sayyaf. Khan was gradually weaned from the JI, and he exclusively allied al-Badr with the Hezb-i-Islami (HIA) led by Gulbuddin Hekmatyar, who today plays a key role in the Afghan resistance. As a result, the JI announced its separation with al-Badr when it launched the Hizbul Mujahideen militant movement in Kashmir in 1989. Al-Badr was kicked out of Afghanistan after the emergence of the Taliban in the mid-1990s because of its affiliation with the HIA. The ISI then set up new camps for al-Badr in Pakistani Azad Kashmir - that portion of Kashmir administered by Pakistan. In the Kargil operation of 1999, which almost brought Pakistan and India to all-out war, al-Badr fighters were initially sent by the Pakistan army to occupy Indian bunkers. Later, another ISI connection, the recently arrested Khalil, and his fighters battled side-by-side with Khan and the Pakistan army against Indian forces".[18]

On 30 September 2020, Express Tribune reported former Prime Minister Nawaz Sharif's warning to PMLN members that parliament had been turned into a "rubber stamp" as he had been told that somebody else was running it instead of the legislators. "How independent is the parliament you are a member of?" the PML-N supreme leader asked while virtually addressing a meeting of the party's Central Executive Committee from London. "We have come out of the slavery of the colonialism only to be enslaved by our own," he claimed. "We are not free citizens... ask yourself if you are a free citizen. The time is not far away when all these things will have to be accounted for. "The convicted former premier said he had decided not to live a life of "humiliation". "If the nation also decides that it has to take a stand against tyrants and oppressors, then the real change will come in a few months and weeks, not years."..."I received a message in the middle of the night," he added. The PML-N supreme leader said he was warned that there would be consequences if he did not step down and martial law could also be imposed. "I said go ahead with whatever you want to do but I won't resign." The newspaper reported.[19]

Daily Express Tribune's News Desk (November 13, 2020) reported Nawaz Sharif's attack against the miltablishment and ISI for their alleged plot to remove him from power. "I cannot blame the entire army for the lawlessness of a few individuals," he said while addressing via video link his Pakistan Muslim League-Nawaz's (PML-N) latest power show in Swat. The Newspaper reported. However, Express Tribune reported Nawaz had for the first time named the army chief and DG ISI, saying that there was "a state above the state" in the country. "My only crime is to talk about the rights of common man, constitution and democratic principles," Nawaz said in today's address. He reiterated that his fight was not against Prime Minister Imran Khan but those "who brought him to power". Meanwhile, his daughter Maryam continued her rhetoric against the incumbent government and said it was a "wall of sand that needs one final push". The Newspaper reported.[20] The ISI and military establishment involvement in manipulating cases in High-courts and Supreme Court against political leaders. Islamabad High Court Judge (India.com News Desk, July 22, 2018) warned that the ISI spy agency has been attempting to control the country's judiciary to get favourable verdicts in different cases including that of Nawaz Sharif. He alleged that ISI has asked the Chief Justice of Pakistan to not let former Chief Minister Nawaz Sharif and his daughter Maryam Nawaz out of jail till the elections. While speaking at the Rawalpindi Bar Association, Islamabad High Court judge, Justice Shaukat Siddiqui, said that ISI has been trying to control the judiciary. "Today the judiciary and media have come under the control of 'Bandookwala' (army). Judiciary is not independent. Even the media is getting directions from the military. The media is not speaking the truth because it is under pressure and has its interests," he said. "In different cases, the ISI forms benches of its choice to get desired results. The ISI had asked the chief justice to make sure that Nawaz Sharif and his daughter Maryam Nawaz should not come out of jail before the July 25 election. It also had asked him not to include me in the bench hearing the appeal of Nawaz Sharif and his daughter in the Avenfield case. The CJ told ISI that he would make a bench of its choice," he said.[21]

The Mumbai attacks introduced the ISI Chief General Pasha as a controversial personality within the intelligence community of South Asia. In 2008, President Asif Ali Zardari had instructed Pasha to go to India to share intelligence after a request from Indian Prime Minister Manmohan Singh, but under pressure from the Pakistan military, the decision was however procrastinated within a few hours. Lt. General Pasha was involved in the memo gate controversy of 2011–2012, in which an American businessman, Mansoor Ijaz alleged that a senior Pakistani diplomat, former Ambassador Husain Haqqani, had asked him to deliver an unsigned memorandum to Admiral Michael Mullen, Chairman of the US Joint Chiefs of Staff at the time. After his retirement, General Pasha took a foreign job, which war criticized by politicians and parliamentarians.[22]

On 02 August 2018, Dawn Newspaper reported anxiousness of the three-member bench, headed by Chief Justice of Pakistan Mian Saqib Nisar, and asked Defence Secretary retired Lt Gen Zamirul Hassan to furnish before the court no-objection certificates issued by the government to former army chief Gen Raheel Sharif and ISI Director General Ahmad Shuja Pasha for joining foreign jobs. The apex court wondered how the top officers of the armed forces, who were at the helm of affairs and privy to sensitive information related to Pakistan's security, could accept jobs in other countries without completing the mandatory two-year period after retirement. A senior government official on condition of anonymity said that Federal Government rules, as well as army rules, disallowed officers from accepting any employment without a minimum gap of two years after retirement or unless an NOC was issued by the federal government granting permission to join such services. The defence secretary, however, explained before the court that no officer in the armed forces held foreign nationality. The court asked him whether or not Lt Gen Pasha accepted a job in the United Arab Emirates (UAE) just a few days after his retirement, whereas Gen Sharif also accepted the post of Commander of Islamic Military Counterterrorism Coalition in the Kingdom of Saudi Arabia. CJP Nisar asked whether or not the ban on job without completing the two-year gap was also applicable to the two officers of the armed forces. The newspaper reported.[23]

The TTP commander Ehsanullah Ehsan (ISI chief begged for Taliban's help in Kashmir, September 6, 2020), who escaped from a safe house operated by the Pakistan army reveals how Pakistan army and the ISI demanded help of various terror groups to target Indian and US forces. Ehsan wrote in The Sunday Guardian from an undisclosed location.[25] Former ISI Chief, General Asim Munir has also been playing the role of vandals and DAKO mafia group by using the ISI officer to terrify business communities in Pakistan. The News intervention in its heart-touching report about the corruption and vandalism of the former Chief of Inter-Services Intelligence (ISI) exposed the real face of Pakistan army and the ISI's sarcastic Director Generals. The news Intervention reported a blatant bribery case of Gujranwala's District senior commander and former ISI Chief General Asim Munir who immediately demanded Rs. 90 crore in extortion money from the CEO of Master Tiles. Former ISI Chief Lieutenant-General Asim Munir had previously held the privileged positions of DG ISI and DG Military Intelligence (MI):

In February 2017, during the Faizabad sit-in Lieutenant General Asim Munir was the ISI Director General. Ironically, Major General Faiz Hameed, who was Deputy Lieutenant General at the time Asim Munir was responsible for the ISI's internal security wing, also faced this judgment but was promoted to lieutenant general and took over the reins of the ISI from Asim Munir. Lt. Gen. Asim Munir was unceremoniously removed from the prime post of ISI Director General and had to pass as the Gujranwala Corps Commander, thus earning the dubious distinction of being the ISI Chief for the shortest period. Asim Munir was now approaching his retirement and in order to earn quick money like other officers in the Pak Army, he contacted Sheikh Mahmood Iqbal, the managing director of Master Tiles, and demanded ninety crores of rupees. Dismayed by this blatant extortion request from Gujranwala Corps Commander Sheikh Mahmood Iqbal, CEO Master Tiles wrote a letter to Prime Minister Imran Khan Niazi, dated June 05, 2021, outlining all the details of his meeting with the lieutenant General Asim Munir and his subsequent request for Rs 90 crore in extortion money".[26] In his letter to Prime Minister Imran Khan Sheikh Mahmood Iqbal, CEO Master Tiles (News Intervention-June 5, 2021) described all the details of what the ISI Chief had told him and his subsequent request for Rs 90 crore in extortion money:

"Lieutenant-General Asim Munir sent me a message from a staff member, Colonel Ehtesham, last Thursday morning, saying he wanted to have lunch with me. I started from a meeting with Japanese importers and went to the cantonment to meet him (Asim Munir). I was offered good food, salmon fish cooked with broccoli and olive oil, among other delicacies. As we sipped black coffee with luxurious Cuban cigars, Lt. Gen. Asim Munir said he discovered that the executive range of our bathroom tiles was being smuggled to the Central Asian countries of Tajikistan and Uzbekistan via the Wakhan corridor in Afghanistan. He then said billions of rupees were being lost in taxes to the national treasury. Of course, this was all a plot to trap me, "New Intervention reported. Sheikh Iqbal complained: "... they seized two of our company's trucks in Peshawar on the Afghan border ... this seizure was carried out in the same way that the anti-narcotics force seized 20 kg fake heroin from the car of Rana Sanaullah, who is a leader of the Pakistan Muslim League. (Midday). Asim Munir told me that in political, commercial and espionage operations, perception is more important than reality, and if perception is imprinted in people's minds that Master Tiles is involved in smuggling, then our share price would fall on the stock markets. I asked Lieutenant-General Asim Munir in a trembling voice what he wanted from me. "Lieutenant General Asim Munir said he wanted five million seven hundred thousand dollars, which equals ninety crore rupees in Pakistani currency. Asim said that if I transferred the money to his bank account in Macau, he would help me smuggle tiles to Central Asia, because Senior Commander Peshawar was his roommate and roommate... " explained the Sheikh. Mahmood Iqbal in his letter. "... if necessary, in order to save my business, I agree to give this kind of money to Lt. Gen. Munir, but how long can we feed these little Fauji Asim snakes." They trample on the constitution every time. Sometimes they torture journalists Asad Ali and Matiullah Jan, other times, through Papa Jones, they set up a smuggled-funded business empire on the Pakistan-Iran border. I ask you to help me with this problem; otherwise, I will move my whole business setup to Dhaka. But then you will have to handle a five thousand crore jobless people in Pakistan. After this incident, I understood that a man loves his self-esteem more than his homeland. The dastardly Satanism and the arrogance of power in those ugly eyes is unbearable. Sometimes when I sleep, this anger wakes me up at night and I have to take some water with aspirin, "said Sheikh Mahmood Iqbal, CEO of Master Tiles in his letter to Imran Khan Niazi". News Intervention reported.[27]

The flagrant and barefaced abrupt retirement of former ISI Chief General Rizwan raised many questions including his brother's illegal business and corruption. General Rizwan abruptly requested for early retirement. In his letter to the army quarters, he asked for "premature release". General Akhtar, replaced by Lt Gen Naveed Mukhtar as Director General (DG) ISI, was posted as President of the National Defence University. The JUI-F's Senator Hafiz Hamdullah said was there any political party which could ask why a seasoned senior general opted for early retirement and what the reasons behind this move were. On 07 October 2017, in his Tweet, Hashim Azam called Lt Gen Rizwan Akhtar as a "butcher of hundreds of Mohajirs & a corrupt General. He should be arrested & trial on Mohajirs killings & corruption". Prominent journalist and writer, Rauf Klasra claimed that "his brother Air Commodore Imran Akhtar who was appointed as Director Procurement and Logistics Department in PIA was also involved in the deal of a PIA aircraft A-310 which resulted in a loss of Rs 500 million". Similarly there are rumours that as DG Rangers Sindh General Rizwan Akhtar was also involved in corruption amounting to billions, though no evidences have been brought so far but his early retirement has raised concerns. Daily Dawn (Military rejects speculation about ISI chief, Baqir Sajjad Syed, 23 February, 2021) reported military spokesman General Iftikhar Babar's clarification that Director General of Inter-Services Intelligence (ISI) Lt General Faiz Hameed will not be changed in the near future.[28]

Chapter 8

Military and Political Stakeholders, Crisis of Confidence and Lack of Modern Intelligence Technique

As the key providers of information relevant to national security threats, agencies are essential components of every state security system. The need for intelligence (Florina Cristiana Matei and Carolyn Halladay-2019) is a fact of life for modern governments. Few states take the view that they can dispense with a foreign intelligence service and none is sufficiently immune from terrorism or the inquisitiveness of its neighbours' to forgo an internal security service.[1] The fact is; intelligence is crucial to the survival of the state and the mandate of a security intelligence service defines the tasks that the service has to perform, and provides the guiding principles by which the service conducts its operations and measures effectiveness.[2] In the wake of recent series of sectarian and terrorist attacks on civilian and military installations, and growing security concerns has been a wave of new security regulation and unlimited power aimed at expanding intelligence powers across the country.[3] The perception that the agencies decide whatever they want without restricting themselves to the advisory role causing misunderstanding between the citizens and the state. Political rivalries, poor coordination, sectarian and political affiliations, uncorroborated reports, and lack of motivation are issues that need the immediate attention of policymakers.[4] Janani Krishnaswamy (2013) in her research paper on the causes of Indian intelligence failure diverted public attention to the starting point of failures:

"Why do our secret intelligence agencies fail repeatedly? It is because of (a) lack of adequate intelligence, (b) dearth of trained manpower in the intelligence sector, (c) lack of proper intelligence sharing between the center and the state, (d) lack of action on available intelligence, (e) the current state of political instability or (f) the lack of sensible intelligence reforms? In the aftermath of the terrorist attack at Dilsukhnagar in

Hyderabad, India's secret intelligence agencies were subjected to an intense inspection. Heated political debates over the construction of the National Counterterrorism Centre (NCTC), a controversial anti-terror hub that was proposed in the aftermath of 26/11 attacks, was stirred up after five years. Are such organisational reforms sufficient to fix the problems of the intelligence community? Intelligence reviews committees and politicians constantly assess the performance of intelligence agencies and underline numerous failures within the intelligence system."[5]

Pakistan army and its intelligence agencies are facing the same challenges on domestic and international fronts. It spends a huge budget on military buildup, and luxurious enjoyment of generals. The fund the military receives from the state budget is in addition to the revenue it gets from its large business operations. Notwithstanding being rich itself, the army continues to be a burden on the country's weak economy. Political instability is endemic to Pakistan with governments alternating between legitimacy and illegitimacy and political leadership propped by the Army, does not have a free hand. That kind of government has never been able to handle economic crisis. Pakistani Writer and analyst Muhammad Taqi (13 March 2019) has painted an under whelming picture the army role in politics in a nutshell: "The problem with the army's obsession with becoming the sole arbiter of national interest and security is that it has arrogated itself the right to dictate domestic and foreign policies to suit that rather nebulous creed in which Pakistan and Islam are somehow in perpetual danger and the army is the only savior they have. These twin delusions of paranoia and grandeur are actually feigned and self-serving to justify the outfit's choke hold on the country and its resources"[6]

The complex reciprocation among the internal and external forces fashioning Pakistan today call on to an in-depth evaluation of their influence on the country's future-in the context of both continued state stability and Pakistan's potential to jump-start broader security priorities in the region. The country maintains 32 secret agencies working under different political and bureaucratic stakeholders but failing to maintain domestic stability and support the culture of intelligence sharing on law enforcement level. Established in 1948, the ISI was tasked with acquiring intelligence of strategic interests and assessing the intensity of foreign threats, but, unfortunately, ISI was tasked by General Zia to vanquish political leadership, make alliances and recruit jihadists for Kashmir and Afghanistan.[7] Civilian intelligence agency (Intelligence Bureau) has been gradually neglected, and phased-down during the consecutive military rule. Military analysts Sanjeeb Kumar Mohanty and Jinendra Nath Mahanty (04 October 2011) in their research paper on the nexus of sectarian takfiri organizations and Pakistan army, highlighted the evolution of ISI during the Zia military regime:

"The 1980s were the years when the CIA-ISI relationship blossomed, and during this period the ISI grew in strength and reach. Further, the realization the nuclear neighbours cannot fight a war without the possibility of its slipping out of control led General Zia to tap the mullahs and madrassas to wage a new covert war in India and Afghanistan". Religious movements, such as Jammat-e-Islami and Tablighi Jammat were allowed by Zia to operate inside army barracks. In fact, the imposition of martial law in Pakistan for the first time in 1958 under General Ayub Khan brought the ISI into political realm. Moreover, Ayub gave the ISI primacy amongst the other intelligence agencies in Pakistan, like the MI (Military Intelligence) and the IB (Intelligence Bureau) because it combined in the one agency the dual roles of internal and external intelligence. The ISI however, concentrated more on internal rather than external intelligence for the first three decades.....Under Zia the ISI grew in size and strength in the power structure due to the dependence of the regime on intelligence and the Afghan operation. From being an implementer of policy, the ISI became the policy maker. In fact, the imposition of martial law in Pakistan for the first time in 1958 under General Ayub Khan brought the ISI into political realm. Moreover, Ayub gave the ISI primacy amongst the other intelligence agencies in Pakistan, like the MI (Military Intelligence) and the IB (Intelligence Bureau) because it combined in the one agency the dual roles of internal and external intelligence. The ISI however, concentrated more on internal rather than external intelligence for the first three decades. Till the seventies, the organization had a limited external agenda which was largely India-centric. This was because Pakistan had fought three wars with India and remained preoccupied with an Indian military threat to her national security"[8]

The military rulers acted like warlords and never thought about security sector reforms to make law enforcement agencies fit to the fight against anti-state elements, extremism and radicalization. They acted for the interests of the United States-criminalized trade and agriculture, supported Talibanization in society, and introduced culture of soldiers for sale in Middle East. The state fostering of surrogate militants to serve Pakistan's strategic interests in Kashmir and Afghanistan played a crucial role in the rise of transnational jihadism.[9] Sanjeeb Kumar Mohanty and

Jinendra Nath Mahanty in their paper also noted all weather relationship between the ISI and extremist organizations in South Asia and Central Asia: "During the 1990s, several Kashmir-specific militant outfits were sponsored by Pakistan. The ISI helped create, mentor, finance and train outfits like Jaish-e-Muhammed (JeM), Harkat-ul-Mujahideen (HuM), Lashkar-e-Tayyeba (LeT) and several other shadowy extremist groups to fight a proxy war against Indian forces in Jammu and Kashmir, admittedly part of the larger Pakistani strategy to bleed India with thousand cuts....... At the end of 1995, it was reported that the ISI in collaboration with the Jammat-e-Islami (Pakistan's oldest religious-political party), was raising a Taliban type force consisting of young students from Pakistan with the sole purpose of fighting Indian forces in Jammu and Kashmir. From the 1990s, the LeT became the ISI's favorite terrorist outfit operating in Kashmir and in the rest of India.........During Musharraf's time, the infamous mullah-military alliance was strengthened even in the face of his growing unpopularity after joining the US-led war on terror. Since 9/11, the Pakistani military has tried to distance itself from militancy in Jammu and Kashmir under intense US and international pressure. The militant groups that had long depended on ISI support described Musharraf's U-turn on Kashmir as a betrayal of their struggle for independence."[10]

Under Muhammad Zia-ul-Haq's leadership, the Inter-Services Intelligence (ISI) grew in strength and resources. The agency received further training from the Unites States in intelligence collection and technology use to effectively counter Russian intelligence in Pakistan. The agency concentrated more on internal rather than external intelligence for the first three decades-discouraged political forces and fostered sectarian mafia groups to protect its own interests abroad. In 1980s, during the Soviet presence in Afghanistan, the ISI's strength became more important for both Pakistan and the United States. The fact is they were on great mission to disintegrate union of the Soviet. Pakistan's army encouraged jihad to throw Russian forces out of Afghanistan, and promoted the interests of the United States and its NATO allies. The ISI got a chance to support its favorite guerrilla groups and co-ordinate the flow of foreign aid, including the recruitment of volunteers and graduates of local madrassas.[11] Researchers and analysts Grant Holt and David H. Gray in their paper (Winter-2011) highlighted the role of ISI during the Zia regime:

"The Afghan war created a leviathan and powerful intelligence agency in the ISI while Zia mandated Islamic fundamentalism and Deobandism (a strict interpretation of the Hanafi school of Sunni Islam) into their shadowy ranks. With aid from the U.S. and a pivotal and violent struggle against the Soviets in Afghanistan, the ISI cultivated a relationship with extremists from across the globe, including al-Qaeda. While being forced to adhere to fundamental Islam from the Pakistani state, the ISI itself became recognized in the international system and feared within domestic society. Throughout the 1990s, the ISI maintained its relationship with extremist networks and militants that it had established during the Afghan war to utilize in its campaign against Indian forces in Kashmir. Many high-profile terrorist incidents, ranging from the September 11, 2001 attacks on New York and Washington to the July 7, 2004 subway bombings in London to the November 2008 assault on Mumbai, have had direct connections to individuals and groups operating in Pakistan (Ganguly and Kapur 47). The sponsorship and recruitment of terrorist and guerilla movements against the Soviets in Afghanistan is paramount when examining historic ties between terrorism and the ISI. However, the agency also took part in, and was responsible for, numerous international operations and violent acts across the globe."[12] The involvement of military in operational mechanism and function of ISI adversely affected the agency's civilian reach. The agency later on was unable to assess the importance of civilian stratification and intelligence strength of neighbouring states. Normally, civilian intelligence is stronger than the military agency as its civilian roots enable it to manage its operational capabilities.[13] Pakistan corrupt political culture forced the agencies to look at the civilian population and government with scorn. They were inculcated that the job of national security is beyond the reach of civilian governments. Rajesh Bhushan (12 January 2019) has assessed the strength of ISI in his well-written analysis:

"Until 2018, Pakistan's Inter Service Intelligence (ISI) had around 6,000 people, which includes its handlers, agents and sources. According to German scholar Hein Kiessling, who represented the Hanns-Seidel-Foundation (Munich) in Pakistan from 1989 to 2002 said, "The (real) ISI budget is top secret, only a few people know the figure". "In fact officially the ISI budget today is between $300 and 400 million." According to Kiessling, the personnel strength of ISI is also considered as top secret. "During Zia-ul Haq's tenure it was estimated to be 20,000 men. In the 1990s and in the new millennium there were drastic reductions in personnel. "Therefore, it is now assumed that ISI's base strength is approximately 4,000. Higher estimates often encountered in literature and the press is grossly exaggerated." Hein Kiessling said changes in personnel policies came out in 2009 under the command of Pakistan Army chief General Ashfaq Parvez Kayani. "Today with the exception of six-seven two-star generals, the military personnel in ISI come from the Intelligence Corps of the army —a move that serves towards the professionalism of the service".[14]

Miltablishment used agencies against politicians and its critics to punish them for criticizing corruption of Generals and their cronies. They punished those who wrote stories of forced disappearances, and torture of innocent writers. The ISI professional approach of intelligence mechanism never improved due to its prolixity of involvement in politics. Dr Bidanda M Chengappa noted some aspects of ISI relationship with Afghan Mujahedeen: "Thereafter from the early 1980s the ISI provided strong support to the Afghan mujahedeen against Soviet occupation forces there and ultimately proved successful due to the material resources provided by the US. It is aptly stated that the victory was possible on account of "American weaponry and Afghan bravery".[15] The import of the ISI involvement in Afghanistan is that the ISI developed close working relations with the CIA and Saudi intelligence organizations. More significantly the ISI developed enormous hands-on expertise to wage a proxy war in terms of handling logistics on an international scale, training Afghan guerillas in low-intensity conflict operations (LICO) and intelligence-gathering activities under hostile conditions. The ISI has developed close linkages with various Islamic fundamentalist organizations like the Lashkar-e-Toiba and Harkat-ul-Mujahideen. The ISI funds their activities like para-military training and procurement of arms to wagc arc against the Indian State. This ISI nexus with fundamentalist parties provides the agency with manpower which can be mobilized as 'street power' to agitate against or support a political party which has taken a decision with national, regional, political, social or economic ramifications.8 To that extent, the ISI has some leverage to influence decision making owing to its ability to operate through fundamentalist parties".[16]

The ISI is no doubt an incompetent intelligence agency, and is a shame of the nation, but military and political leadership used it against political opponents. This policy of both political and military establishments destroyed the professional capabilities of the agency. The agency was often used against IB and used against journalists and human rights activists, and then used against politicians and FIA. In his research paper, Dr Bidanda M Chengappa has argued that ISI was mainly controlled and used by military against democratic government in Pakistan. There are articles and research papers in international press about the business of ISI and its darling organizations in Afghanistan, Iran and India: "Apparently the ISI is controlled either by the military or the political leadership depending on whichever is in power. The DG-I, as the head of the ISI is known, is an appointment made by the Prime Minister in consultation with the Chief of Army Staff (COAS). The DG-I reports to the Prime Minister considering the ISI has a political section to handle internal intelligence duties. However the army appears to dictate the policy towards India even when the country has an elected leader. To that extent it would be appropriate to state that the PM has a degree of control over the ISI's involvement in internal affairs which the Chief of Army Staff oversees the external role of the agency. The rationale for the evolution of the intelligence service into an extra-constitutional power center is multi-faceted and encompasses military strategy, martial law, involvement in the clandestine nuclear programme, covert support to para-military operations in the Afghan jihad and linkages with fundamental parties. While some of these causes have internal dimensions, some are completely external".[17]

In books and newspapers, there are stories about the failure of intelligence agencies in Pakistan to undermine terrorism and extremism. Recruitment from the business community, wealthy and landlord societies, generals and politicians for intelligence agencies prompted bureaucratic culture. Intelligentsias and political circles have often pointed to the fact that involvement of the agency in political confrontations badly affected its professional credibility. Some circles are trying to radicalize agencies, but the big concern is that all military, civilian and policing agencies have already 'purified' their souls in Tablighi congregations in Raiwand. Sectarian elements within the IB and ISI ranks are purveying secret information about the planning of political parties and military leadership, to their favourite religious and political leaders. Secondly, military intelligence agencies do not cooperate with civilian intelligence agencies on national security issues. The ISI never extended a hand of cooperation to civilian intelligence agencies, or even considered IB as an older civilian brother, over the past five decades. Analyst Taha Siddiqui (06 May 2019) noted some aspects of the ISI involvement in politics:

"Domestically, he is known to have manipulated Pakistani politics both covertly and overtly and was instrumental in doing so in his last stint during the era of General Pervez Musharraf who ruled Pakistan from 1999 to 2008. Internationally, he is known to have linkages with jihadist organizations, including al-Qaeda, the Afghan Taliban as well as Kashmir and India-focused groups.......When Musharraf imposed martial law on October 12, 1999, Brigadier Shah was the director of the Inter-Services Intelligence (ISI) in Punjab, Pakistan's largest and politically dominant province. Thus he became an important ally in the general's attempt at reshaping the politics of the region. Under Shah, the Intelligence Bureau became Musharraf's eyes and ears. It reported directly to the military dictator and helped him continue a countrywide 'political engineering' project. But it's not just political manipulation under General Musharraf that Brigadier Shah is known for. He was also the key to the rapid Talibanisation of the tribal belt next to the Pak-Afghan border, when Pakistan joined the so-called War on Terror in Afghanistan, led by the United States of America and its ally's post 9/11. The most incriminating allegation against Shah yet is by the assassinated former Prime Minister Benazir Bhutto, who first named him as one of the suspects behind the suicide bombing targeting her on arrival in October 2007 in the city of Karachi. Bhutto survived the attack that left at least 180 people dead. She named him again in a letter made public after her death, saying Brigadier Shah should be investigated if she were assassinated. Bhutto had alleged that Shah was conspiring with terrorists to carry out her assassination".[18] The CIA influence on the ISI operational mechanism and domestic policy making causing misunderstanding between civilian and military stakeholders. The agency's reluctant cooperation with law enforcement agencies, and its grudging intelligence sharing with naval and air agencies, also caused disappointment among different stakeholders. On 01 August 2001, Indian analyst B. Raman in his research paper (No-287), noted some aspects of the evolution of ISI during the Zia-ul-Haq regime:

"Zia-ul-Haq expanded the internal intelligence responsibilities of the ISI by making it responsible not only for the collection of intelligence about the activities of the Sindhi nationalist elements in Sindh and for monitoring the activities of Shia organizations all over the country after the success of the Iranian Revolution in 1979, but also for keeping surveillance on the leaders of the Pakistan People's Party (PPP) of Mrs. Benazir Bhutto and its allies which had started the Movement for the Restoration of Democracy (MRD) in the early 1980s. The ISI's Internal Political Division had Shah Nawaz Bhutto, one of the two brothers of Mrs. Benazir Bhutto, assassinated through poisoning in the French Riviera in the middle of 1985, in an attempt to intimidate her into not returning to Pakistan for directing the movement against Zia, but she refused to be intimidated and returned to Pakistan. The Afghan war of the 1980s saw the enhancement of the covert action capabilities of the ISI by the CIA. A number of officers from the ISI's Covert Action Division received training in the US and many covert action experts of the CIA were attached to the ISI to guide it in its operations against the Soviet troops by using the Afghan Mujahideen, Islamic fundamentalists of Pakistan and Arab volunteers".[19]

Since the departure of Pervez Musharraf in 2008, the military pledged its commitment to protecting democracy. Yet it has consistently undermined civilian governments to maintain military prerogatives and, if not establish direct control of the state, but the ISI is still controlled by the army, and never allowed it to help democratic governments in the process of economic and political stabilization. The IB is under resources, while its leadership has retrieved policing training, and acts like a police officer. There is an opposition between law enforcement and intelligence, because the two entities are very different. In his research paper, Dr Bidanda M Chengappa has argued that ISI is mainly controlled and used by military against democratic government in Pakistan:

"Apparently the ISI is controlled either by the military or the political leadership depending on whichever is in power. The DG-I, as the head of the ISI is known, is an appointment made by the Prime Minister in consultation with the Chief of Army Staff (COAS). The DG-I reports to the Prime Minister considering the ISI has a political section to handle internal intelligence duties. However, the army appears to dictate the policy towards India even when the country has an elected leader. To that extent, it would be appropriate to state that the PM has a degree of control over the ISI's involvement in internal affairs which the Chief of Army Staff oversees the external role of the agency. The rationale for the evolution of the intelligence service into an extra-constitutional power center is multi-faceted and encompasses military strategy, martial law, involvement in the clandestine nuclear programme, covert support to para-military operations in the Afghan jihad and linkages with fundamental parties. While some of these causes have internal dimensions some are completely external".[20]

The unending resultant tussle between civilian and military intelligence agencies forced former Prime Minister Nawaz Sharif to restructure the IB and make it more effective to counter ISI's influence in political institutions. The Prime Minister allocated huge funds to the IB to recruit and employ more agents to meet the country's internal and external challenges. The greatest challenge Nawaz Sharif faced was on the national security front. The miltablishment was not happy with his national security approach.The Intelligence Bureau is the country's main civilian intelligence agency, and functions under the direct control of the Prime Minister, tackling terrorism, insurgency and extremism. Over the last four decades, the ISI operated in changing security environment, but it mostly targeted democracy and political parties, strengthened miltablishment and its illegal business. The ISI, the MI and the IB assumed more controversial proportions than ever before. Journalist and expert Abbas Nasir (Herald, January 1991) describes the way intelligence targets politician in many ways to retrieve information:

"On a freezing December day in Islamabad, MNA Dr. Imran Farooq, ordered the maintenance staff of the MNA hostel to service his room heater. The staff took down the gas heater, only to discover a device that didn't belong there taped to its back. Noticing that there were batteries attached to it, they immediately became alarmed and summoned the bomb disposal squad. Being experts at their job, the members of the bomb squad soon allayed the perturbed MNA's fears that the device was not a bomb of any sort. Instead, they said, they had discovered a powerful transmitter that was being used to bug the MQM MNA's room. While the federal interior minister was quick to order an inquiry into the affair, the MQM blamed the former PPP government for bugging Dr. Farooq's room. The real culprit, however, is still to be identified. A few days earlier, a heated debate in parliament had focused on the activities of our intelligence agencies as being "rather over-extended". As the range of intelligence operations came under discussion, the fact that their agencies were maintaining files and tapes - not only on all politicians in the country, but many non-political civilians as well - drew the wrath of many MNAs of all political shades. Finally, Speaker Gohar Ayub tried to round up the debate, not only by ordering a select committee to look into the matter, but also admitting that "we have all been the target of intelligence agencies."[21]

Abbas Nasir is a senior journalist who knows how Pakistani intelligence agencies were spying on citizens and politician, and how they violated their right of privacy. The evolution of ISI through different states made the agency capable to adopt professional approach in countering national security threats. Former Prime Minister Zulfiqar Ali Bhutto was the only person who realized the importance of a strong and competent intelligence agency in enhancing the goal of foreign policy. Abbas Nasir noted the zeal of Mr. Bhutto to make professionalize:

"According to him, Bhutto chose the ISI to be the premier agency because he could accomplish two tasks with it. The first related to the country's foreign policy and the second to self-preservation, as only a services intelligence agency could look into the army itself and keep Bhutto abreast with the mood and the sentiment in the forces. This part of history also had its ironical twists. It is widely believed that Bhutto promoted General Zia as the army chief, superseding several far more senior and well-reputed lieutenant generals, because the DG of the ISI had recommended him as the most "reliable and loyal" choice for the coveted post. It was no coincidence then, that when Bhutto was overthrown, Lt General Ghulam Jilani was retained as the DG of the ISI. Jilani remained one of the most trusted Zia lieutenants for a number of years, both as DG and later as the governor of Punjab. While Jilani was the governor of Punjab, he made a decision that would create obstacles in the path of the PPP for years to come. He plucked a young industrialist from relative obscurity and nurtured him as a civilian alternative to the PPP leadership. The young man would be prime minister one day. To this day, Jilani remains Nawaz Sharif's key mentor".[22]

Prime Minister Benazir Bhutto strengthened the role of the Intelligence Bureau (IB) to collect intelligence information for her government, and used it against opposition parties and ISI as well. There has been a clash of interest between the ISI and the IB management in 1990s. Both the ISI and IB were trying to get the favour of Prime Minister. Prime Minister Benazir created 20 senior positions at the joint director level to strengthen the management structure in the organization. Dr. Bidanda M. Chengappa explains the role of ISI and IB against civilian government in Pakistan: "In post–Zia Pakistan, intelligence agencies were effectively used to topple governments. One such case pertains to how an intelligence agency was used to remove then Prime Minister Benazir Bhutto from office. It has been reported that on July 17, 1989 an intelligence agency clandestinely recorded the conversation between then Prime Ministers Benazir and Rajiv Gandhi while the latter was on a state visit to Pakistan. The room was bugged by the intelligence agency and the two leaders in the course of their private meeting at Islamabad discussed, among other issues, the possibility of mutual troop reduction. Apparently, Benazir was supposed to have agreed in principle to the proposal. Soon thereafter, the Chief of Army Staff (COAS) General Mirza Aslam Beg and President Ghulam Ishaq Khan met each other on July 24, 1989 and decided to topple the Benazir government. In order to convince the Opposition and obtain their backing for the need to destabilize the government these tapes were reportedly played to them. 20 It essentially had the desired effect and successfully influenced the Opposition parties to side with the COAS and the President against Benazir Bhutto".[23]

In 2008, President Asif Ali Zardari ordered the military's spy agency, the Inter-Services Intelligence (ISI) to be put under the control of the Interior Ministry, but within 24 hours, the President had to withdraw his orders. The ISI's primary aim (Shuja Nawaz-2011) has been 'counterintelligence and espionage, especially aimed at India, where it has been fairly successful, but the IB was countering political parties. Prominent analyst B.Raman in his paper highlighted political confrontation, and the role of army in overthrowing democratic government. Prime Minister Nawaz Sharif warned Mullah Omer to stop supporting Sepah Sahaba and cooperate with the United States. The army didn't like this way of treating their proxies by the Prime Minister. B.Raman has noted aspects of the whole saga:

"The third instance was during the second tenure of Nawaz Sharif (1997-99) when his action in appointing Lt. Gen. Ziauddin, an engineer, as the DG ISI, over-riding the objection of Gen. Musharraf led to the first friction between the two. Gen. Musharraf transferred Lt. Gen.Mohammad Aziz, the then DDG ISI on his promotion as Lt. Gen. to the GHQ as the CGS and transferred the entire Joint Intelligence North (JIN), responsible for covert actions in India and Afghanistan to the Directorate-General of Military Intelligence (DGMI) to be supervised by Lt. Gen.Aziz. It is believed that the JIN continues to function under the DGMI even after the appointment of Lt. Gen. Mahmood Ahmed as the DG, ISI, after the overthrow of Sharif on October 12, 1999. Gen. Musharraf, as the COAS, stopped inviting Lt. Gen. Ziauddin to the Corps Commanders conferences. He kept Lt. Gen. Ziauddin totally out of the picture in the planning and implementation of the Kargil operations. After the Kargil war, Nawaz Sharif had sent Lt.Gen.Ziauddin to Washington on a secret visit to inform the Clinton Administration officials of his concerns over the continued loyalty of Gen. Musharraf".[24] Prime Minister Nawaz Sharif experienced the same challenges as a head of the IJI-led government which also resorted to using intelligence agencies to gain unfair advantage in domestic politics. The IB spied on MQM leaders and installed intelligence monitors devices in their rooms and houses. However, Nawaz Sharif also killed Army Chief General Asif Nawaz Janjua and FIR was filed against Brigadier Imtiaz, the Director of Intelligence Bureau (DIB). The General's wife Nuzhat Janjua's formal complaint to the then President Ghulam Ishaq Khan about the unnatural death of her husband raised several important questions. Dr. Bidanda M. Chengappa has noted some important aspects of General Asif Nawaz Janjua murder:

"Nuzhat Janjua suspected that her late husband had been poisoned with arsenic administered in a cup of tea served to him at a meeting of the Joint Chiefs of Staff Committee meeting. Some political commentators have also pointed out that his widow must have made the formal complaint on the basis of some strong grounds and that the bereaved lady would not make such an attempt for political purposes. Interestingly the government posted a police picket at the general's grave in order to ensure that the body was not exhumed for medical inspection. There were rumors that the general's stomach was removed prior to the burial to avoid detection of foul play. The issue snowballed in April 1993 as the Army adopted an open-minded approach to the possibility of foul play behind the general's death. The rationale for discussing General Asif Nawaz Janjua's death in such great detail is only because if the conspiracy theory is valid then the tacit role of intelligence agencies is bound to assume relevance. To that extent this could well be one more instance of intelligence agencies interfering in internal politics. The incident illustrates how even an Army chief was vulnerable to the machinations of the intelligence agencies despite the power that is associated with his office".[25]

Pakistani intelligence agencies have been shaping governments, parliaments, and dissolve it while the interests of military establishment is not served. This is a catchphrase, and a verbalism appearing in newspapers and intellectual debates since 1980s. International media have also published numerous articles that highlighted the role of intelligence agencies in politics and judicial matter in Pakistan. I am not going to discredit ISI or criticize the IB to make my debate engrossing, because ISI is a professional intelligence agency of the country, and the IB stakeholders need to fix some cleft in the wall. On 22 October 2019, Dr Niaz Murtaza in his article sternly criticized military rulers and their involvement in politics. Dr. Murtaza also argued that policies of dictators caused extremism and social alienation; "Zia ruled for 11 years with absolute powers, guided by security-phobic lenses and with little regard for public welfare. Obviously, it would take highly capable rulers with a concern for public welfare, long tenures and full powers to undo this harm. No civilian has had the longevity or full powers to do so. His army successor Musharraf had these luxuries. But despite his enlightened moderation mantra, his policies turned Zia-era extremism into huge terrorism as he too was guided by security-phobic rather than public welfare lenses. Today, Pakistan has a sullied global reputation. The economy is industrially stagnant and suffers large deficits and debt. Politics suffers from instability, corruption, incompetence and agencies' control. Society is bigoted and intolerant with little space for freedom of thought and speech. All these reflect the corrosion of basic societal structures and the undermining of social, political, economic and national capacities primarily under Zia".[26]

Notes to Chapters

Introduction

1. Friday Times Najam Sethi, 15 July 2022
2. The Nation, 02 July 2022
3. Hindustan Times, 02 July 2022
4. Pakistan National Commission for Human Rights NCHR
5. Association of Electronic Media Editors and News Directors (AEMEND)
6. 21 April 2022, the Committee to Protect Journalists
7. The International Federation of Journalists
8. Tracking Civic Space (Monitor-16, 08 2022
9. Ibid
10. Sanskriti Bhatnagar, (Press freedom in Pakistan has the latest casualty the arrest of ARY News journalist: Pakistan ranks 157 on the Reporters Without Border's Press Freedom Index of 2022, below war-torn Afghanistan and Russia, the Print, 10 August, 2022).
11. Ibid
12. Ibid
13. The news 19 August 2022
14. Express Tribune, 18 August 2022
15. Najam Sethi in his editorial comment, 15 August 2022
16. MM News (15 August 2022
17. WION TV channel in its report, 18 August 2022
18. Ibid
19. Dawn. 18 August 2022
20. Canadian Parliamentarian, Tom Kmiec accused him for supporting terrorist groups. Visiting Canada, General Qamar Javed Bajwa came under heated criticism in the Canadian Parliament. Mr. Tom Kmiec who slammed his government for approving the amount of $50,000 for COAS Bajwa's reception from the taxpayer money of Canada. Mr. Kmiec said Bajwa was accused of

toppling two civilian governments. Adding that military under his command was accused of human rights abuses, and extrajudicial killings, and has deep links to terrorist groups.

21. Newspaper Dawn reported agreement of PTI and PMLN (Rare consensus among rivals on ISI's role in civilian setup-June 4, 2022
22. Outlook Magazine of India 07 August 2022
23. Declan Walsh book "The Nine Lives of Pakistan".
24. Expert and journalist, Mr. Abbas Nasir has documented. 14 September 2017

Chapter 1: Pakistan in the Eye of a Thunderstorm

1. Expert and analyst, retired Indian Army Officer who has served in terrorism-infested areas of Jammu & Kashmir, Assam, Nagaland and Manipur, Nilesh Kunwar (June 26, 2022.
2. Global Village Space in its news analysis. 29 November 2017
3. MEMRI-TV, Tehreek Labbaik Ya Rasool Allah-TLY: The Islamist Movement At The Center Of Anti-Government Protests In Pakistan-November 27, 2017
4. Expert and analyst, Mosharraf Zaidi in his column. How TLP won 2017, 2018, 2020 and 2021: Since the Faizabad dharna, the TLP leadership has figured out a formula that makes their speeches, their Facebook posts and their WhatsApp messages more powerful-The News, 02 November, 2021.
5. The Dawn Newspaper. 06 February 2019
6. October 30, 2021, The Friday Times
7. Pakistan Today October 26, 2021
8. Expert and analyst, Sushant Sareen in his research paper. Tehrik-E-Labbaik Pakistan: The New Face of Barelvi Activism. Occasional Paper No. 332, September 2021, Observer Research Foundation.
9. Researcher on Strategic and Economic Affairs and Consultant with the National Security Council Secretariat (NSCS) Vaishali Basu Sharma in her recent analysis. Tehreek-e-Labbaik Pakistan: A Case of the Military Losing Control over Islamists-20 April 2021.
10. The Print, 20 April, 2021
11. Sushant Sareen in his research paper. Tehrik-E-Labbaik Pakistan: The New Face of Barelvi Activism-Occasional Paper, 15 September, 2021, Observer Research Foundation
12. Umer Farooq in his article (For Pakistan's Security Establishment, Lal Masjid Is Not The Problem, Abdul Aziz knows how to attract Pakistan's media with emotional sloganeering and how to galvanize militant groups.12The Friday Times, 28 September 2021

13. The Friday Times, 28 September 2021
14. Mullah Abdul Aziz of Red Mosque Islamabad in his recent interview with a local journalist (Quran orders to become terrorists: Maulana Abdul Aziz, SAMVADA-25 August 2021) communicated that the Holy Quran had ordained Muslims to become terrorists against enemies of Allah.
15. The Holy Quran never instructed or directed Muslims to become terrorists against the enemies of Allah Almighty. The Quran says: "When it is said to them: "Make no mischief on the earth," They say: "Why we only want to make peace. Of a surety, they are the ones who make mischief, but they realize (it) not". Al Baqara, 2:11
16. Mrityunjoy Kumar Jha in his analysis (India Narrative, 09-12-2021
17. Expert Assaf Moghadam (Suicide Terrorism, Occupation, and the Globalization of Martyrdom: A Critique of Dying to Win, published in 2006
18. Analyst and writer, Florian Weig has noted (Afghanistan's Taliban: Legitimate Jihadists or Coercive Extremists?)
19. Global Witness research report
20. 10 June 2022, Human Rights Watch report
21. Human Rights Watch on 07 July 2022

Chapter 2: The Army, Agencies and Political Alliances

1. October 2021, News-18
2. Newspaper Dawn reported (Rare consensus among rivals on ISI's role in civilian setup-June 4, 2022) concordance of PML-N and PTI—that the country's premier spy agency, the Inter-Services Intelligence (ISI), should be under civilian control and answerable to the parliament after the PML-N-led coalition government gave the agency legal cover to screen civilian officials.
3. Newspaper Dawn reported (Rare consensus among rivals on ISI's role in civilian setup-June 4, 2022
4. Outlook Magazine of India in its report (Pakistan Government Formally Assigns Govt Officials' Screening to Spy Agency ISI: 07 August 2022
5. Senior Fellow in IDSA, Dr. Bidanda M. Chengappa in an article: The ISI Role in Pakistan's Politics
6. Ibid
7. 25 January 2022, Dawn newspaper
8. 29 January 2022, Friday Times
9. Mrityunjoy Kumar Jha. 16-01-2022
10. World News 17 February 2022
11. 12 June 2022 the Guardian

12. 05 June 2022, The Week Magazine's Web Desk. Pakistan: Demand to hold ISI accountable unites political rivals: Agency has been authorised to screen public officials.

13. 05 July 2022, the Hindu newspaper

Chapter 3: How and why Tablighi Jamaat became a Major Intelligence Infrastructure of International Political and Military Stakeholders?

1. A unit of Aadhyaasi Media and Content Services Private Limited, OpIndia it its news commentary (Tablighi Jamaat and its links to terrorist organizations: History of association to Al Qaeda, Taliban and Kashmiri terrorists: Secret US documents released by Wikileaks in 2011 revealed that some Al Qaeda operatives used the Jamaat to get visas and fund their travel to Pakistan. They also lived in and around Delhi, the documents said-31 March, 2020.

2. 07 July 2005, London bombings were facilitated (Mohammed Siddique Khan and Shahzad Tanweer) by Tablighi Jamaat, Stratfor.

3. Experts and analysts, Fred Burton and Scott Stewart in their report. Tablighi Jamaat: An Indirect Line to Terrorism-The Stratfor January 23, 2008

4. Arsalan Khan in his recent research paper. Contested Sovereignty: Islamic Piety, Blasphemy politics and the paradox of Islamization in Pakistan-08 Jun 2022

5. South Asia Democratic Forum in its research paper (Policy Brief 10–Tablighi Jamaat and its role in the Global Jihad. South Asia Democratic Forum 11 December 2020.

6. Ibid

7. Ibid

8. Ibid

9. Vaibhav Singh's Tweet (04 April 2020

10. Journalist Qaiser Butt reported to Express Tribune (Islamabad refuses to hand over ex-ISI chief to Bosnia tribunal: The Hague earlier demanded custody of Lt Gen Javed Nasir for his alleged support to Muslim fighters in the 1990s war-September 20, 2011.

11. Hindustan Times (Pakistan stood in support of Tablighi Jamaat, is Imran Khan going against Saudi Arabia? 24 December 2021

12. Ashwaq Masoodi (16 September 2013

13. Al Jazeera news. Pakistan quarantines 20,000 following Tabligh gathering in Lahore, 6 Apr 2020

14. Business Standard, 02 April 2020

15. Eurasia Daily Monitor. The Tablighi Jamaat: A Soft Islamization from the Ferghana Valley to Russia's Turkic Regions? The Jamestown Foundation's Eurasia Daily Monitor Volume: 10 Issue: 12, 2013
16. Sushant Sareen in his recent article. The Tablighi Jamaat tangle, Observer Research Foundation-01 April 2020
17. The BBC news report. Tablighi Jamaat: The group blamed for new Covid-19 outbreak in India-02 April 2020
18. Telangana Today A shake-up for Central Asia-14 January 2022
19. Francesca Marino. Quint, 21 Jan 2022
20. Salahuddin Shoaib Choudhury in his article. Pakistani ISI uses Tablighi Jamaat for spreading Islamist jihad, Organizer Newspaper, 28 Dec, 2021.
21. EU today news report (Europe & US terror fears over Tablighi Jamaat Islamic group, 26 August 2020
22. Diplomat, 11 January 2022
23. Dr. Afsana Mammadova noted (Kazakhstan on the threshold: geostrategic competition or geopolitical reality, Modern diplomacy. January 12, 2022
24. Luca Anceschi, professor of Eurasian Studies. Carnegie Europe, 11 January 2022

Chapter 4: Imran Khan, Military Establishment and the Inter-Services Intelligence

1. Non-resident scholar in the South Asia Program at the Carnegie Endowment for International Peace, James Schwemlein
2. Press Trust of India (24 June 2022
3. Ibid
4. Dibakar Dutta, (10 April, 2022
5. 17 July 2022, Dawn newspaper
6. F.M. Shakil in his article (The growing 'tug-of-war' between Pakistan's spy agencies: Conflict between the civilian Intelligence Bureau (IB), and the military's Inter-Services Intelligence (ISI) is at boiling point, with the former accused of overstepping constitutional bounds, Asia Times. 04 October 2017.
7. February 2020, Ehsanullah
8. The Sunday Guardian (06 September, 2020
9. Ibid

Chapter 5: The ISI Political Role and its War against Civilian Intelligence

1. 2019, BBC report
2. 19 March 2012, the News International

3. The Nation 2019
4. Masud Ahmad Khan, Targeting state institutions, the nation April 05, 2021
5. Prominent analyst and writer, Farhatullah Babar in 10 July 2012 moved a bill to control ISI or bring it under democratic control.
6. 10 July 2012, the News International
7. 16 May 2014, the News International
8. 16 May 2014, the News International reported the Intelligence Bureau (IB) proposal of oversight law to watch performance of intelligence agencies
9. 25 July 2015, the News
10. 28 February 2018, Umar Cheema of the News International Lahore
11. Ibid, Omer Cheema
12. Middle East Institute, November 3, 2020
13. 11 July 2013, the News International
14. Ibid
15. Ibid
16. 09 January, 2021, Times of India

Chapter 6: Politicians dancing to the ISI's Jitterbug

1. Financial Times-12 January 2012
2. 01 July 2013, Dawn newspaper
3. Dawn newspaper on 07 March, 2013
4. Musa Khan Jalalzai, 2015
5. Pakistan's Inter-Services Intelligence Contributes to Regional Instability. Global Security Review, Alexandra Gilliard-Jun 7, 2019, and the Challenges of Civilian Control over Intelligence Agencies in Pakistan, Frederic Grare, 18 December 2015. Book Chapter: Bangladesh Institute of Law and International Affairs.
6. John. R. Schmidt, ISI Wrongfully Accused of Killing Journalist? Also Pakistan's Supreme Court told military and intelligence agencies to stay out of politics, Agence France-Presse, 07 Feb, 2019Agence France-Presse, 07 February 2019
7. Digital Desk of Sentinel (19 September 2020) has noted multirole stories of the ISI in Pakistan, and quoted journalist's Declan Walsh book to uncover misgivings of the agency approach to national security and neighbouring states.
8. Ibid
9. Alamedas papers, 26 January 2020, Dawn newspapers

10. Ibid
11. Ibid
12. Express Tribune newspaper (26 April 2017)
13. DAWN 06 October, 2016
14. Dawn 14 October 2016
15. 12 October 2016, DAWN newspaper
16. October 2016, a columnist for Dawn newspaper, Cyril Almeida, wrote a front-page story about a rift between Pakistan's civilian and military leaderships over militant groups that operate from Pakistan but engage in proxy war against India and Afghanistan.
17. 10 June 2017, the Wire
18. Scholar Frederic Grare (18 December 2015)
19. Pakistan: Living with Nuclear Monkey. 2018
20. Ibid
21. 06 October 2016, Dawn newspaper reported an unprecedented warning of civilian government to the military leadership of a growing international isolation of Pakistan and sought consensus on several key actions by the state.
22. Ayaz Amir (daily Dawn. 22 September 2006
23. Ibid
24. 07 May 2018; Javid Ahmad

Chapter 7: War Criminals and Pilferers

1. Amit Chaturvedi, of Hindustan Times-31, 2021 has quoted the daily Mail letter narrating the presence of those in the court who committed crimes.
2. Research Fellow, Institute for Conflict Management, Ajit Kumar Singh noted that 'though just two weeks have passed since the Taliban returned to power in Kabul, fear among masses, as expected, has spread like wildfire across Afghanistan, forcing thousands to run towards the Hamid Karzai International Airport in Kabul, to escape a dreaded future.
3. Shaun Gregory (ISI and the War on Terrorism. Studies in Conflict & Terrorism Volume: 30 Issue-12, December 2007
4. On 12 March, 2021 (ToloNews) journalist Haseeba Atakpal once more defined the role of ISI in the Afghan conflict
5. Former terrorist leader and member of TTP spokesman Ehsanullah Ehsan revealed that Pakistan army asked him to lead death a squad. On 13 August 2020, he revealed that Pakistani authorities had given him a hit list of people who they would like to be killed in Khyber Pakhtunkhwa. In an audio, he

claimed that after some time of his surrender he was given the list of prominent voices in order to facilitate Pakistan in eliminating rogue elements.

6. Journalist and Analyst, Kunwar Khuldune Shahid, The diplomat--April 20, 2020

7. The Sunday Guardian (06 September, 2020

8. Ibid

9 Musa Khan Jalalzai, 2018 India,and F. M. Shakil, "The growing 'tug of war' between Pakistan's Spy Agencies", Asia Times, October 4, 2017, http://www.atimes.com/article/growing-tugwar-pakistans-spy-agencies/.

10. M. Ilyas Khan (Uncovering Pakistan's secret human rights abuses, BBC News, Dera Ismail Khan, 2 June 2019.

11. 16 August 2015, DW news

12 15 August 2015, BBC

13. Analyst Shekhar Gupta (25 May 2018

14 Abbas Nasir, "Pakistan's Intelligence Agencies: The inside Story"

15. Pakistan Press International on 15 May 2005, reported the PPP reference against the ISI DG Lieutenant General Javed Nasir.

16. G Parthasarathy, Rogue army runs the show-11 January, 2003, The Pioneer

17. In an interview with the BBC in August 2015, Senator Mushahidullah Khan claimed that an audio tape obtained by the Intelligence Bureau was played during a meeting between Prime Minister Nawaz Sharif and Raheel Sharif

18. 19-Aug-04, Asia Times

19. 30 September 2020, Express Tribune

20. Daily Express Tribune's News Desk (November 13, 2020) reported Nawaz Sharif's attack against the miltablishment and ISI for their alleged plot to him from power

21. Musa Khan Jalalzai, 2018

22. Dr Niaz Murtaza. Dawn. 22 October, 2019

23. 02 August 2018, Dawn Newspaper reported anxiousness of the three-member bench, headed by Chief Justice of Pakistan Mian Saqib Nisar.

24. The TTP commander Ehsanullah Ehsan (ISI chief begged for Taliban's help in Kashmir, September 6, 2020) who escaped from a safe house operated by the Pakistan army reveals how Pakistan army and the ISI demanded help of various terror groups to target Indian and US forces.

25. Joint Intelligence Directorate", National Counter Terrorism Authority NACTA Pakistan, Government of Pakistan, https://nacta.gov.pk/jointintelligence-directorate-jid/.

26. Former ISI Chief, Lt. General. Asim Munir has also been playing the role of vandals and DAKO mafia group by using the ISI officer to terrify business communities in Pakistan. The NEWintervention in its heart-touching report about the corruption and vandalism of former Chief of Inter-Services Intelligence (ISI) exposed the real face of Pakistan army and the ISI's sarcastic Director Generals. The news Intervention reported a blatant bribery case of Gujranwala's District senior commander and former ISI Chief, Lt. General. Asim Munir who immediately demanded Rs. 90 crore in extortion money from the CEO of Master Tiles. Former ISI Chief Lieutenant-General Asim Munir had previously held the privileged positions of DG ISI and DG Military Intelligence (MI).
27. In his letter to Prime Minister Imran Khan Sheikh Mahmood Iqbal, CEO Master Tiles (News Intervention-June 5, 2021) described all the details of what the ISI Chief had told him and his subsequent request for Rs 90 crore in extortion money.
28. On 07 October, 2017, in his Tweet, Hashim Azam called Lt Gen Rizwan Akhtar as a "butcher of hundreds of Mohajirs & a corrupt General.

Chapter 8: Military and political Stakeholders, Crisis of Confidence and lack of Modern Intelligence Technique.

1. Rai Mansoor Imtiaz (14 November 2019
2. Ibid
3. Intelligence war in Afghanistan, 2018
4. Florina Cristiana Matei and Carolyn Halladay-2019
5. Ibid
6. Ibid
7. Dr. Julian Richards, an author of four books and a number of papers and book chapters on a range of security and intelligence issues have contributed a chapter on Pakistan's intelligence agencies in the book (The Image of the Enemy: Intelligence Analysis of Adversaries Since 1945.
8. Prem Mahadevan research paper. 2011
9. Janani Krishnaswamy. 2013
10. Pakistani Writer and analyst Muhammad Taqi. 13 March 2019
11. Military analysts Sanjeeb Kumar Mohanty and Jinendra Nath Mahanty, 04 October 2011
12. Sanjeeb Kumar Mohanty and Jinendra Nath Mahanty
13. Grant Holt and David H. Gray in their paper, Winter-2011
14. Rajesh Bhushan, 12 January 2019

15. Dr Bidanda M Chengappa noted some aspects of ISI relationship with Afghan Mujahedeen.
16. Ibid
17. Dr Bidanda M Chengappa
18. Analyst Taha Siddiqui, 06 May 2019
19. 01 August 2001, Indian analyst B.Raman
20. Dr Bidanda M Chengappa
21. Abbas Nasir. Herald, January 1991
22. Ibid
23. Dr. Bidanda M. Chengappa
24. 01 August 2001, Indian analyst B.Raman
25. Dr. Bidanda M. Chengappa
26. 22 October 2019, Dr Niaz Murtaza

Bibliography

Ahady Anwar-ul-Haq. 1991. Conflict in post-soviet-occupation Afghanistan. Journal of Contemporary Asia, Vol. 21, No. 4

Abbas, Hassan 2015. Pakistan's Drift into Extremism: Allah, the Army, and America's War Terror. Abingdon: Routledge.

Afzal, Madiha 2018. Pakistan under Siege: Extremism, Society, and the State. Washington, DC: Brookings Institution Press.

Ahmed, Shamila Kouser, 2012, July. The Impact of the "War on Terror": On Birmingham's Pakistani Kashmiri Muslims' Perceptions of the State, the Police and Islamic Identities. (Doctoral Thesis, University of Birmingham, Birmingham, United Kingdom). http://etheses.bham.ac.uk/id/eprint/3635

Ali, Murad, 2012.The Politics of Development Aid: The Allocation and Delivery of Aid from the United States of America to Pakistan. Doctoral Thesis, Massey University, Palmerston North, New Zealand. URL: http://hdl. handle.net/10179/3418

Ahmed, Khaled. 2016, Sleepwalking to Surrender: Dealing with Terrorism in Pakistan. Haryana: Viking. Ataöv, Türkkaya (2018): Kashmir and Neighbors: Tale, Terror, Truce.

Abingdon: Routledge. Barfield, Thomas. 1996. 'The Afghan Morass', Current History, Vol. 95, No. 597.

Andrew, Christopher M. and Jeremy Noakes. 1987. Intelligence and International Relations, 1900-1945. Exeter: Exeter University Press,

Ashman, Harold Lowell. 2009. Intelligence and Foreign Policy: A Functional Analysis. Salt Lake City: Ashman, 1974. Association of the Bar of the City of New York, Committee on Civil Rights The Central Intelligence Agency: Oversight and Accountability. New York,

Abshire, David. 2001, "Making the Pieces Fit: America Needs a Comprehensive National Security Strategy." American Legion Magazine,

Ackerman, Wystan M. 1998,"Encryption: A 21st Century National Security Dilemma." International Review of Law, Computers & Technology.

Andersen, Per, Richard Morris, David Amaral, Tim Bliss, & John O'Keefe 2006. The Hippocampus Book, Oxford: University Press.

Anderson, Alan Ross, & Nuel D. Belnap, Jr. 1975 Entailment: The Logic of Relevance and Necessity, Princeton University Press, Princeton.

Anderson, John R. (1983) The Architecture of Cognition, Cambridge, MA: Harvard University Press.

Anderson, John R., & Gordon H. Bower,1973 Human Associative Memory, Washington, DC: Winston.

Anderson, John R., & Gordon H. Bower, 1980 Human Associative Memory: A Brief Edition, Hillsdale, NJ: Erlbaum.

Anderson, John R., & Lebiere, C. 1998. The atomic components of thought, Mahwah, NJ: Erlbaum.

Adams, Thomas K. "Future Warfare and the Decline of Human Decisionmaking." Parameters, Winter 2001/2002, v. 31, no. 4

Adler, Emanual. "Executive Command and Control in Foreign Policy: The CIA's Covert Activities," Orbis, fall 1979, v. 23, no. 3

Agrell, Wilhelm. Sweden and the Dilemmas of Neutral Intelligence Liaison. Journal of Strategic Studies, August 2006, v. 29, no. 4

Aid, Matthew M. "All Glory is Fleeting: SIGINT and the Fight against International Terrorism." Intelligence and National Security, Winter 2003, v. 18, no. 4

Ast, Scott Alan. Managing Security Overseas: Protecting Employees and Assets in Volatile Regions Boca Raton; FL: CRC Press, 2010.

Ataov, Türkkaya 2018: Kashmir and Neighbors: Tale, Terror, Truce. (Routledge Revivals). Abingdon: Routledge.

Afghanistan Analyst Network (Osman, B.) 18 October 2019, The Islamic State in 'Khorasan': How it began and where it stands now in Nangarhar, 27 July 2016, https://www.afghanistan-analysts.org/the-islamic-state-inkhorasan-how-it-began-and-where-it-stands-now-in-nangarhar/,

Amnesty International, Pakistan: Enduring Enforced Disappearances, 27 March 2019,https://www.amnesty.org/en/latest/research/2019/03/pakistan-enduring-enforceddisappearances/, accessed 15 July 2019

Azam, M., Javaid, U, 2017, The sources of Militancy in Pakistan, in: Journal of the Research Society of Pakistan, Volume No. 54, Issue No. 2 http://pu.edu.pk/images/journal/history/PDF-FILES/13-Paper_54_2_17.pdf, accessed 24 July 2019.

Baloch, H., Peace Talks, ISKP and TTP--The Future in Question, 6 May 2019, ITCT (Islamic Theology of Counter Terrorism), https://www.itct.org.uk/wp-content/uploads/2019/05/Peace-Talks-ISKP-andTTP.

Bell, Paul M. P. 2007, Pakistan's Madrassas – Weapons of Mass Instruction? (Master's Thesis, Naval Postgraduate School, Monterey, United States). URL: http://hdl.handle.net/10945/3653

Bennett, John T. 2014, Bend but Don't Break: Why Obama's Targeted-Killing Program Challenges Policy and Legal Boundaries but Rarely Breaches them. (Master's Thesis, Johns Hopkins University, Baltimore, United States). http://jhir.library.jhu.edu/handle/1774.2/37221

Badalic, Vasja, 2019 The War against Civilians: Victims of the "War on Terror" in Afghanistan and Pakistan.(Palgrave Studies in Victims and Victimology). Cham: Palgrave Macmillan / Springer Nature. DOI: https://doi.org/10.

Bergen, Peter L.; Rothenberg, Daniel (Ed.) 2015, Drone Wars: Transforming Conflict, Law, and Policy. New York: Cambridge University Press.

Bergen, Peter L.; Tiedemann, Katherine (Eds.), 2013, Talibanistan: Negotiating the Borders between Terror, Politics, and Religion. Oxford: Oxford University Press. Brooke-Smith, Robin (2013): S

Bayly, C. A. 1996, Empire and Information: Intelligence Gathering and Social Communication in India: 1780-1880. NY: Cambridge University press,.

Bazan, Elizabeth B. 2008. The Foreign Intelligence Surveillance Act: Overview and Modifications. New York: Nova Science Publishers,

Bailey, David, 1997, A Computational Model of Embodiment in the Acquisition of Action Verbs, Doctoral dissertation, Computer Science Division, EECS Department, University of California, Berkeley.

Baillie, Penny, 2002 The Synthesis of Emotions in Artificial Intelligence, PhD Dissertation, University of Southern Queensland.

Baker, Mark C. 2003 Lexical Categories: Verbs, Nouns, and Adjectives, Cambridge University Press, Cambridge.

Baldwin, J.F. 1986 Automated fuzzy and probabilistic inference, Fuzzy Sets and Systems, vol 18,

Ballard, Dana H., Mary M. Hayhoe, Polly K. Pook, & Rajesh P. N. Rao 1997 Deictic codes for the embodiment of cognition, Behavioral and Brain Sciences 20, 723-767.

Bar Hillel, Yehoshua, 1954 Logical Syntax and Semantics, Language 30, 230-237.

Beck, Melvin. 1984. Secret Contenders: The Myth of Cold War Counterintelligence. New York, NY: Sheridan Square Publications,

Beichman, Arnold. 1984. "The U.S. Intelligence Establishment and Its Discontents." IN Dennis L. Bark (ed.) To Promote Peace: U.S. Foreign Policy in the Mid-1980s. Stanford, CA: Hoover Institution Press, Stanford University,

Bazai, Fida Muhammad, 2016 Pakistan's Responses to the United States' Demands in the War against the Taliban and Al-Qaeda. (Doctoral Thesis, University of Glasgow, Glasgow, United Kingdom). http://encore.lib.gla.ac.uk/iii/encore/record/C-Rb3258590

Bell, Paul M. P. (2007, March): Pakistan's Madrassas – Weapons of Mass Instruction? (Master's Thesis, Naval Postgraduate School, Monterey, United States). URL: http://hdl.handle.net/10945/3653

Bennett, John T. 2014 Bend but Don't Break: Why Obama's Targeted-Killing Program Challenges Policy and Legal Boundaries but Rarely Breaches them. (Master's Thesis, Johns Hopkins University, Baltimore, United States). http://jhir.library.jhu.edu/handle/1774.2/37221

Bhattacharya, Sandhya S. 2008 The Global Impact of Terror: 9/11 and the India-Pakistan Conflict. (Doctoral Thesis, Pennsylvania State University, State College, United States https://etda.libraries.psu. edu/catalog/7900

Barrett, David M. "Glimpses of a Hidden History: Sen. Richard Russell, Congress, and Oversight of the CIA." International Journal of Intelligence and Counterintelligence, Fall 1998, v. 11, no. 3, p. 271-298.

Barry James A. "Managing the Covert Political Action: Guideposts from Just War Theory." Studies in Intelligence, 1992, v. 36, no. 5 https://www.cia.gov/library/center-for-the-study-of-intelligence/kentcsi/docs/v36i3a05p_0001.htm

Barry, James A. Bridging the Intelligence-Policy Divide. Studies in Intelligence, 1994, v. 37, no. 5. https://www.cia.gov/library/center-for-the-study-of-intelligence/kentcsi/docs/v37i3a02p_0001.htm

Basile, James F. Congressional Assertiveness, Executive Authority and the Intelligence Oversight Act: A New Threat to the Separation of Powers. Notre Dame Law Review, 1989, v. 64, no. 4

Beres, Louis Rene. On Assassination, Preemption, and Counterterrorism: The View from International Law." International Journal of Intelligence and Counterintelligence, Winter 2008, v. 21, no. 4

Bhattacharya, Sandhya S. 2008, The Global Impact of Terror: 9/11 and the India-Pakistan Conflict. (Doctoral Thesis, Pennsylvania State University, State College, United States). https://etda.libraries.psu. edu/catalog/7900

Clarke, Ryan 2011, Crime–Terror Nexus in South Asia: States, Security and Non-State Actors. (Asian Security Studies). Abingdon: Routledge.

Coll, Steve, 2018 Directorate S: The C.I.A. and America's Secret Wars in Afghanistan and Pakistan. New York: Penguin Press.

Dorronsoro, Gilles. 2012. 'The transformation of the Afghanistan-Pakistan border', in under the drones: Modern lives in the Afghanistan-Pakistan Borderlands. Harvard University Press

Cassirer, Ernst,1942 Zur Logik der Kulturwissenschaften, translated by S. G. Lofts as The Logic of the Cultural Sciences, Yale University Press, New Haven.

Cattell, R. G. G., & Douglas K. Barry, eds. 1997, The Object Database Standard, ODMG 2.0, Morgan Kaufmann, San Francisco, CA.

Ceccato, Silvio. 1961 Linguistic Analysis and Programming for Mechanical Translation, Gordon and Breach, New York.

Ceccato, Silvio,1964 Automatic translation of languages, Information Storage and Retrieval 2:3, 105-158.

Chafe, Wallace L. 1970 Meaning and the Structure of Language, University of Chicago Press, Chicago.

Chamberlin, Don, 1996 Using the New DB2, Morgan Kaufmann Publishers, San Francisco.

Cruickshank, Paul, 2013, Al Qaeda. (5 Vols.). (Critical Concepts in Political Science). Abingdon: Routledge.

Canfield, Robert L. 1992. 'Restructuring in Greater Central Asia: Changing Political Configurations', Asian Survey, Vol. 32, No. 10.

Drumbl, Mark A. 2002. 'The Taliban's 'other' crimes', Third World Quarterly, No. 23.

Daily Times, Police service-challenges and reforms, 6 October 2018,https://dailytimes.com.pk/306595/police-service-challenges-and-reforms/,

Daily Times, Reforming the judicial system, 8 March 2019,https://dailytimes.com.pk/362536/reforming-the-judicial-system/, accessed 17 October 2019

Dawn, 2009: Southern Punjab extremism battle between haves and have-nots, 21 May 2011 https://www.dawn.com/news/630651, accessed 21 July 2019

David, G.J. 2009. Ideas as Weapons: Influence and Perception in Modern Warfare. Washington, DC: Potomac Books,

DCAF Intelligence Working Group, Intelligence Practice and Democratic Oversight – a Practitioner's View. DCAF, Occasional paper no. 3. August 2003.

Dehaene, Stanislas, 2014 Consciousness and the Brain, New York: Viking.

DeJong, Gerald F.1979 Prediction and substantiation, Cognitive Science, vol. 3,

DeJong, Gerald F. 1982 An overview of the FRUMP system, in W. G. Lehnert & M. H. Ringle, eds., Strategies for Natual Language Processing, Erlbaum, Hillsdale, NJ,

Deledalle, Gerard, 1990 Charles S. Peirce, Phénoménologue et Sémioticien, translated as Charles S. Peirce, An Intellectual Biography, Amsterdam: John Benjamins.

de Moor, Aldo, Wilfried Lex, & Bernhard Ganter, eds. 2003 Conceptual Structures for Knowledge Creation and Communication, LNAI 2746, Berlin: Springer.

Deng, Li, & Dong Yu, 2014 Deep Learning: Methods and Applications, Foundations and Trends in Signal Processing.

Dennet, Daniel C. 1987 The Intentional Stance, MIT Press, Cambridge.

Dennet, Daniel C. 1995 Darwin's Dangerous Idea: Evolution and the Meanings of Life, Simon & Schuster, New York.

Dennet, Daniel C. 1996 Kinds of Minds, New York: Basic Books.

Dearth, Douglas H. 1992, Strategic Intelligence and National Security: A Selected Bibliography. Carlisle Barracks, PA: U.S. Army War College Library, http://handle.dtic.mil/100.2/ADA256389

Dearth, Douglas H. and R. Thomas Goodden. 1995. Strategic Intelligence: Theory and Application. 2nd ed. Carlisle Barracks, PA: U.S. Army War College Library

Der Derian, James. 1992. Antidiplomacy: Spies, Terror, Speed and War. Cambridge, MA: Blackwell,

Diamond, John. 2008.The CIA and the Culture of Failure: U.S. Intelligence from the End of the Cold War to the Invasion of Iraq. Stanford, CA: Stanford Security Series,

Dawn, Military courts cease to function today, 31 March 2019,https://www.dawn.com/news/1472947, accessed 3 July 2019

Dawn, Military Courts part of National Action Plan: PM Nawaz, 30 December 2014https://www.dawn.com/news/1154046, accessed 20 July 2019

Diplomat, July 2019,The, Taking Stock of Pakistan's Counterterrorism Efforts, 4 Years After the Army Public School Attack, 21 December 2018, https://thediplomat.com/2018/12/taking-stock-of-pakistanscounterterrorism-efforts-4-years-after-the-army-public-school-attack/,

Economic Times (The), US asks Pakistan to act against Haqqani network, other terror groups, 27 February 2018, https://m.economictimes.com/news/defence/us-asks-pak-to-act-against-haqqaninetwork-other-terror-groups/articleshow/63096010.cms, accessed 17 June 2019

Express Tribune, The Army launches Operation Radd-ul-Fasaad against terrorists across the country,22 February 2017, https://tribune.com.pk/story/1335805/army-launches-country-wide-operationterrorists/, accessed 30 July 2019

Einstein, Albert, 1921 The Meaning of Relativity, Princeton University Press, Princeton, NJ, fifth edition, 1956.

Einstein, A., H. A. Lorentz, H. Weyl, & H. Minkowski, 1923 The Principle of Relativity, Dover Publications, New York.

Einstein, Albert, 1944 Remarks on Bertrand Russell's Theory of Knowledge, in P. A. Schilpp, ed., The Philosophy of Bertrand Russell, Library of Living Philosophers.

Eklund, Peter W., Gerard Ellis, & G. Mann, eds. 1996 Conceptual Structures: Knowledge Representation as Interlingua, LNAI 1115, Berlin: Springer,

Express Tribune (The), Blast hits Hazara community's shoe market in Quetta, 6 August 2019, https://tribune.com.pk/story/2029583/1-least-two-martyred-13-injured-quetta-market-blast/

Elahi, N. 2019 Terrorism in Pakistan: The Tehreek-e-Taliban Pakistan (TTP) and the Challenge to Security. London: I.B. Tauris.

Fair, C. Christine 2014 fighting to the End: The Pakistan Army's Way of War. Oxford: Oxford University Press.

Fair, C. Christine 2018 In their Own Words: Understanding Lashkar-e-Tayyaba. London: Hurst.

Farwell, James P. 2011 The Pakistan Cauldron: Conspiracy, Assassination & Instability. Dulles: Potomac Books.

Feldman, J. A. 1981. A connectionist model of visual memory. In Hinton, G. E. and Anderson, J. A., editors, Parallel Models of Associative Memory, chapter 2. Erlbaum, Hillsdale, NJ.

Fukushima, K. 1975. Cognitron: A self-organizing multilayered neural network. Biological Cybernetics, 20:121–136.

Feigenbaum, Edward A., & Pamela McCorduck, 1983. The Fifth Generation, Addison-Wesley, Reading, MA. Brain and Language 89, 385-392.

Feldman, Jerome A. 2006 From Molecule to Metaphor: A Neural Theory of Language, MIT Press, Cambridge, MA.

Feldman, Jerome, & Srinivas Narayanan,2004 Embodied meaning in a neural theory of language, Brain and Language 89, 385-392.

Feldman, Jerome, Ellen Dodge, & John Bryant,2009. Embodied construction grammar, in B. Heine & H. Narrog, eds., The Oxford Handbook of Linguistic Analysis, Oxford: University Press.

Fellbaum, Christiane, 1998. WordNet: An Electronic Lexical Database, MIT Press, Cambridge, MA.

Feynman, Richard, 1965 The Character of Physical Law, Cambridge, MA: MIT Press.

Glatzer, Bernt. 2002. 'Centre and Periphery in Afghanistan: New Identities in a Broken State', Sociologus, winter issue.

Goodson, Larry. 1998. 'The Fragmentation of Culture in Afghanistan', Alif: Journal of Comparative Poetics, No. 18, Post-Colonial Discourse in South Asia.

Goodson, Larry P. 1998 'Periodicity and intensity in the Afghan War', Central Asian Survey, Vol. 17, No. 3.

Goudarzi, Hadi. 1999. 'Conflict in Afghanistan: Ethnicity and Religion', Ethnic Studies Report, Vol. XVII, No. 1.

Harpviken, Kristian Berg. 1997. 'Transcending nationalism: the emergence of non-state military formations in Afghanistan', Journal of Peace Research, Vol. 34, No. 3.

Haqqani, Husain, 2018 Reimagining Pakistan: Transforming a Dysfunctional Nuclear State. Noida: HarperCollins India.

Hayes, Louis D. 2016 The Islamic State in the Post-Modern World: The Political Experience of Pakistan. Abingdon: Routledge.

Hiro, Dilip, 2012 Apocalyptic Realm: Jihadists in South Asia. New Haven: Yale University Press.

Hussain, Rizwan, 2005 Pakistan and the Emergence of Islamic Militancy in Afghanistan. Aldershot: Ashgate.

Hinsley, F.H. and Richard Langhorn. 1985, Diplomacy and Intelligence during the Second World War: Essays in Honour of F.H. Hinsley. Cambridge, NY: Cambridge University Press

Hitchcock, Walter T. 1991, The Intelligence Revolution: A Historical Perspective: Proceedings of the Thirteenth Military History Symposium, U.S. Air Force Academy, Colorado Springs, Colorado, October 12-14, 1988. Washington, DC: U.S. Office of Air Force History,

Haaparanta Leila, 1994, Charles Peirce and the Drawings of the Mind, in Histoire Épistémologie Langage 16:1, 35-52.

Harris, Kathryn E. 2015, Asymmetric Strategies and Asymmetric Threats: A Structural-Realist Critique of Drone Strikes in Pakistan, 2004-2014. (Master's Thesis, Virginia Polytechnic Institute and State University, Blacksburg, United States).http://hdl.handle.net/10919/64516

Hoyt, Melanie Raeann, 2014, Decembe. A Game of Drones: Comparing the U.S. Aerial Assassination Campaign in Yemen and Pakistan. (Master's Thesis, Angelo State University, San Angelo, United States).http://hdl. handle.net/2346.1/30273

Hubbard, Austen, 2016, A Study on the Relationship between Security and Prosperity in Pakistan. (Master's Thesis, Angelo State University, San Angelo, United States). URL: http://hdl.handle.net/2346.1/30604

Hussain, Syed Ejaz, 2010, Terrorism in Pakistan: Incident Patterns, Terrorists' Characteristics, and the Impact of Terrorist Arrests on Terrorism. (Doctoral Thesis, University of Pennsylvania, Philadelphia, United States). https://repository.upenn.edu/edissertations/136

Hoffman, Bruce. Lessons of 9/11. Santa Monica, CA: RAND, 2002. http://www.rand.org/pubs/testimonies/CT201/index.html

Hussain, Safdar, and Muhammad Ijaz Latif. 2012. 'Issues and Challenges in Pakistan-Afghanistan Relations after 9/11', South Asian Studies, Vol. 27, No. 1.

Hussain, Shabir, and Syed Abdul Siraj. 2018. 'Coverage of Taliban conflict in the Pak–Afghan press: A comparative analysis', International Communication Gazette.

ICG. 2014. 'Resetting Pakistan's Relations with Afghanistan', International Crisis Group.

Iqbal, Khalid. 2015. 'Natural Allies: TurkeyPakistan-Afghanistan', Defence Journal, Vol. 18. No. 8.

Inderfurth, Karl F. and Loch K. Johnson. 1988, Decisions of the Highest Order: Perspectives on the National Security Council. Pacific Grove, California: Brooks/Cole,.

Ibrahimi, S. Yaqub. 2017. 'The Taliban's Islamic Emirate of Afghanistan (1996–2001): 'War-Making and State-Making' as an Insurgency Strategy', Small Wars & Insurgencies, Vol. 28, No. 6.

Intelligence Services and Democracy. Geneva, Switzerland: Geneva Centre for Democratic Control of Armed Forces, 2002.

Iran: Intelligence Failure or Policy Stalemate? Washington, DC: Georgetown University, Institute for the Study of Diplomacy, 2005. http://www12.georgetown.edu/sfs/isd/Iran_WG_Report.pdf

Jinnah Institute. 2013. 'Sources of Tension in Afghanistan & Pakistan: Perspectives from the Region

Johnson, Thomas H. and M. Chris Mason. 2008. 'No Sign until the Burst of Fire: Understanding the Pakistan-Afghanistan Frontier', International Security, Vol. 32, No. 4.

Jaffrelot, Christophe (Ed.), 2016, Pakistan at the Crossroads: Domestic Dynamics and External Pressures.

(Religion, Culture, and Public Life). New York: Columbia University Press.

Jamal, Arif, 2009, Shadow War: The Untold Story of Jihad in Kashmir. New York: Melville House.

Jan, Faizullah, 2015, The Muslim Extremist Discourse: Constructing Us versus Them. Lanham: Lexington Books.

Jalalzai Musa Khan. May 2018, Pakistan: Living with a Nuclear Monkey, Vij Books India Pvt Ltd, Darya Ganj New Delhi, India,

Judah, Tim. 2002. 'The Taliban Papers', Survival, Vol. 44, No. 1.

Jaffrelot, Christophe, 2016, Pakistan at the Crossroads: Domestic Dynamics and External Pressures. New York: Columbia University Press.

Jalalzai Musa Khan, 22 September, 2015. The Prospect of Nuclear Jihad in Pakistan: The Armed Forces, Islamic State, and the Threat of Chemical and Biological Terrorism. Algora Publishing, Riverside, New York, USA. ISBN-10: 1628941650. ISBN-13: 978-1628941654.

Jan, Faizullah, 2015, The Muslim Extremist Discourse: Constructing Us versus Them. Lanham: Lexington Books.

Kalia, Ravi, 2016, Pakistan's Political Labyrinths: Military, Society and Terror. Abingdon: Routledge.

Kapur, S. Paul, 2017, Jihad as Grand Strategy: Islamist Militancy, National Security, and the Pakistani State. New York: Oxford University Press.

Khalilzad, Zalmay. 1996. 'Afghanistan in 1995: Civil War and a Mini-Great Game', Asian Survey, Vol. 36, No. 2.

Khan, Ijaz. 1998. 'Afghanistan: A geopolitical study', Central Asian Survey, Vol. 17, No. 3.

Magnus, Ralph H. 1998. 'Afghanistan in 1997: The War Moves North', Asian Survey, Vol. 38, No.2.

Maley, William. 1997. 'The Dynamics of Regime Transition in Afghanistan', Central Asian Survey, Vol. 16, No. 2.

Malik, Iftikhar Haider, 2005, Jihad, Hindutva and the Taliban: South Asia at the Crossroads. Karachi: Oxford University Press.

Malik, Jamal, 2008, Madrasas in South Asia: Teaching Terror? (Routledge Contemporary South Asia Series, Vol. 4). Abingdon: Routledge.

Murphy, Eamon, 2013, The Making of Terrorism in Pakistan: Historical and Social Roots of Extremism. (Routledge Critical Terrorism Studies). Abingdon: Routledge.

Murphy, Eamon, 2019, Islam and Sectarian Violence in Pakistan: The Terror Within. Abingdon: Routledge.

Maloney, Sean M. 2015. 'Army of darkness: The jihadist training system in Pakistan and Afghanistan, 1996-2001', Small Wars & Insurgencies, Vol. 26, No. 3.

Mukhopadhyay, Dipali. 2012. 'The Slide from Withdrawal to War: The UN Secretary General's Failed Effort in Afghanistan, 1992', International Negotiation, Vol. 17, No. 3.

Nester, William, 2012, Hearts, Minds, and Hydras: Fighting Terrorism in Afghanistan, Pakistan, America, and Beyond – Dilemmas and Lessons. Dulles: Potomac Books.

Nielsen, Thomas Galasz; Syed, Mahroona Hussain; Vestenskov, David, 2015, Counterinsurgency and Counterterrorism: Sharing Experiences in Afghanistan and Pakistan. Copenhagen: Royal Danish Defence College.

Ollapally, Deepa M. (2008): The Politics of Extremism in South Asia. Cambridge: Cambridge University Press.

Odom, William E. 2003, Fixing Intelligence: For a More Secure America. New Haven: Yale University Press, 2003.

Odom, William E. 2004, Fixing Intelligence: For a More Secure America. 2nd ed.New Haven, CT: Yale University Press, 2004.

Odom, William E. et al. 1997, Modernizing Intelligence: Structure and Change for the 21st Century. Fairfax, VA: National Institute for Public Policy,

Olmsted, Kathryn S. 1996, Challenging the Secret Government: The PostWatergate Investigation of the CIA and FBI. Chapel Hill: University of North Carolina Press,

Olmsted, Kathryn Signe. 1993, Challenging the Secret Government: Congress and the Press Investigate the Intelligence Community, 1974-76. Dissertation. Davis, CA: University of California, Davis.

Pande, Aparna, 2018, Routledge Handbook of Contemporary Pakistan. Abingdon: Routledge.

Rais, Rasul Bakhsh. 2000. 'Afghanistan: A Forgotten Cold War Tragedy', Ethnic Studies Report, Vol. XVIII, No. 2.

Rieck, Andreas. 1997. 'Afghanistan's Taliban: An Islamic Revolution of the Pashtuns' in Orient, Vol. 38, No. 1.

Roy, Olivier. 1992. 'Political elites in Afghanistan: rentier state building, rentier state wrecking', International Journal of Middle East Studies, No. 24.

Rashid, Ahmed, 2008, Descent into Chaos: The United States and the Failure of Nation Building in Pakistan, Afghanistan, and Central Asia. New York: Viking.

Rashid, Ahmed, 2012, Pakistan on the Brink: The Future of America, Pakistan, and Afghanistan. New York: Viking.

Riedel, Bruce, 2011, Deadly Embrace: Pakistan, America, and the Future of the Global Jihad. Washington, DC: The Brookings Institution Press.

Riedel, Bruce, 2013, Avoiding Armageddon: America, India, and Pakistan to the Brink and Back. (Brookings Focus Books). Washington, DC: Brookings Institution Press.

Rubin, Barnett R. 2000. 'The Political Economy of War and Peace in Afghanistan', World Development, Vol. 28, No. 10.

Rubin, Barnett R. 1999. Afghanistan under the Taliban', Current History, Vol. 98, No. 625.

Rubin, Barnett R. 1994. Afghanistan in 1993: abandoned but surviving'Asian Survey, Vol. 34, No. 2.

Schmidt, John R. 2011, The Unraveling: Pakistan in the Age of Jihad. New York: Farrar, Straus and Giroux.

Shah, Sikander Ahmed, 2015, International Law and Drone Strikes in Pakistan: The Legal and Socio-Political Aspects. Routledge Research in the Law of Armed Conflict

Sharma, Surinder Kumar; Behera, Anshuman, 2014, Militant Groups in South Asia. New Delhi: Pentagon Press.

Sheikh, Mona Kanwal, 2016, Guardians of God: Inside the Religious Mind of the Pakistani Taliban. New Delhi: Oxford University Press.

Saikal, Amin. 1996. 'The UN and Afghanistan: A Case of Failed Peacemaking Intervention', International Peacekeeping, Vol. 3, No. 1.

Shahrani, M. Nazif. 2002. 'War, Factionalism, and the State in Afghanistan', American Anthropologist, Vol. 104, No. 3.

Schneider, Erich B. 2013, Balancing the Trinity: U.S. Approaches to Marginalizing Islamic Militancy in Pakistan. Master's Thesis, Naval Postgraduate School, Monterey, United States. http://hdl.handle. net/10945/39008

Shabab, Asma (2012, May): Marketing the Beard: The Use of Propaganda in the Attempt to Talibanize Pakistan. Master's Thesis, University of Southern California, Los Angeles, United States. http://digitallibrary.usc. edu/cdm/ref/collection/p15799coll3/id/38217

Shah, Abid Hussain, 2007,The Volatile Situation of Balochistan – Options to Bring it into Streamline. Master's Thesis, Naval Postgraduate School, Monterey, United States. http://hdl.handle.net/10945/10280

Siddique, Osman, 2013, Rational Irrationality: Analysis of Pakistan's Seemingly Irrational Double Game in Afghanistan. Master Thesis, University of Oslo, Oslo, Norway. https://www.duo.uio.no/ handle/10852/37342

Shahrani, M. Nazif. 2001. 'Resisting the Taliban and Talibanism in Afghanistan: Legacies of a Century of Internal Colonialism and Cold War Politics in a Buffer State', Perceptions: Journal of International Affairs, Vol. 5, No. 4.

Shahrani, M. Nazif. 2000. 'The Taliban Enigma: Person-Centered Politics & Extremism in Afghanistan', ISIM Newsletter, Vol. 6.

Tankel, Stephen, 2013, Storming the World Stage: The Story of Lashkar-e-Taiba. Oxford: Oxford University Press.

Topich, William J. 2018, Pakistan: The Taliban, Al Qaeda, and the Rise of Terrorism. Praeger Security International. Santa Barbara: Praeger.

Tripathy, Amulya K.; Pandit, D. Santishree; Kunjur, Roshni, 2016, Understanding Post 9/11 Cross-Border Terrorism in South Asia: U.S. and other Nations' Perceptions. New Delhi: Ess Ess Publications.

Tarzi, Shah M. 1993. 'Afghanistan in 1992: A Hobbesian State of Nature', Asian Survey, Vol. 33, No. 2.

Verkaaik, Oskar, 2004, Migrants and Militants: Fun and Urban Violence in Pakistan.Princeton Studies in Muslim Politics. Princeton: Princeton University Press.

Vandenbroucke, Lucien S. Perilous Options: Special Operations as an Instrument of U.S. Foreign Policy. New York: Oxford University Press,

Violia, Marc Anthony. 1993. A Spy's Résumé: Confessions of a Maverick Intelligence Professional and Misadventure Capitalist. Lanham, MD: Scarecrow Press

Volkman, Ernest. 1989. Secret Intelligence. New York: Doubleday,

Von Hassell, Agostino. 2006. Alliance of Enemies: The Untold Story of the Secret American and German Collaboration to End World War II. New York: Thomas Dunne Books,

Williams, Brian Glyn. 2014. 'Afghanistan after the Soviets: From jihad to tribalism', Small Wars & Insurgencies, Volume 25, Issue 5-6.

Webel, Charles; Tomass, Mark, 2017, Assessing the War on Terror: Western and Middle Eastern Perspectives. Contemporary Terrorism Studies. Abingdon: Routledge.

Woods, Chris, 2015, Sudden Justice: America's Secret Drone Wars. London: Hurst.

Yasmeen, Samina, 2017, Jihad and Dawah: Evolving Narratives of Lashkar-e-Taiba and Jamat ud Dawah. London: Hurst.

Yusuf, Moeed, 2008, Insurgency and Counterinsurgency in South Asia: Through a Peacebuilding Lens. Washington, DC: United States Institute of Peace Press.

Zaidi, Syed Manzar Abbas, 2016, Terrorism Prosecution in Pakistan. USIP Peaceworks, No. 113 https://www.usip.org/publications/2016/04/terrorism-prosecution-pakistan

Zaidi, Syed Manzar Abbas, 2016, Reconstituting Local Order in Pakistan: Emergent ISIS and Locally Constituted Shariah Courts in Pakistan. (Brookings Local Orders Paper Series, Paper 4). https://www. brookings.edu/research/reconstituting-local-order-in-pakistan-emergent-isis-and-locally-constituted shariah-courts-in-pakistan.

Index

About the Author

Musa Khan Jalalzai is a journalist and research scholar. He has written extensively on Afghanistan, terrorism, nuclear and biological terrorism, human trafficking, drug trafficking, and intelligence research and analysis. He was an Executive Editor of the Daily Outlook Afghanistan from 2005-2011, and a permanent contributor in Pakistan's daily *The Post*, *Daily Times*, and *The Nation*, *Weekly the Nation*, (London). However, in 2004, US Library of Congress in its report for South Asia mentioned him as the biggest and prolific writer. He received Masters in English literature, Diploma in Geospatial Intelligence, University of Maryland, Washington DC, certificate in Surveillance Law from the University of Stanford, USA, and diploma in Counter terrorism from Pennsylvania State University, California, the United States.

CPSIA information can be obtained
at www.ICGtesting.com
Printed in the USA
LVHW042248101022
730382LV00003B/12